MIND AND BODY

OR
MENTAL STATES AND PHYSICAL CONDITIONS

WILLIAM WALKER ATKINSON

SALMON BOOKS

44, Nallathambi St,
Triplicane
Chennai 600005
www.learnerpress.com

ISBN: 978-81-979425-0-1

CONTENTS

FOREWORD

Mind and Body—Mental States and Physical Conditions! To the mind of those who have contented themselves with merely the superficial aspects of things, these two things—mind and body; and mental states and physical conditions—seem to be as far apart as the two poles; seem to be opposites and contradictories impossible of reconciliation. But to those who have penetrated beneath the surface of things, these two apparent opposites are seen to be so closely related and interrelated—so blended and mingled together in manifestation—that it is practically impossible to scientifically determine where the one leaves off and the other begins. And so constant and close is their mutual action and reaction, that it often becomes impossible to state positively which is the cause and which the effect.

In the first place, Science now informs us that in all living substance, from cell to mam moth, there is and must be Mind. There can be no Life without Mind. Mind, indeed, is held to be the very "livingness" of Life—the greater the degree of manifestation of Mind, the higher the degree of Life. Moreover, the New Psychology informs us that upon the activities of the Subconscious Mind depend all the processes of physical life—that the Subconscious Mind is the essence of what was formerly called the Vital Force—and is embodied in every cell, cell-group or organ of the body. And, that this Subconscious Mind is amenable to suggestion, good and evil, from the conscious mind of its owner, as well as from outside. When the subject of the influence of Mental States upon Physical Conditions is studied, one sees that the Physical Condition is merely the reflection of the Mental State, and the problem seems to be solved, the mystery of Health and Disease solved. But in this, as in everything else, there is seen to be an opposing phase—the other side of the shield. Let us look at the other side of the question:

Just as we find that wherever there is living substance there is Mind, so do we find that we are unable to intelligently consider Mind unless as embodied in living substance. The idea of Mind, independent of its substantial embodiment, becomes a mere abstraction impossible of mental imaging—something like color independent of the colored substance, or light without the illuminated substance. And just as we find that Mental States influence Physical Conditions, so do we find that Physical Conditions influence Mental States. And, so the problem of Life, Health and Disease once more loses its simplicity, and the mystery again deepens. The deeper we dig into the subject, the more do we become impressed with the idea of the universal principle of Action and Reaction so apparent in all phenomena. The Mind acts upon the Body; the Body reacts upon the Mind; cause and effect become confused; the reasoning becomes circular—like a ring it has no beginning, no end; its beginning may be any place we may prefer, its ending likewise.

The only reconciliation is to be found in the fundamental working hypothesis which holds that both Mind and Body—both Mental States and Physical Conditions—are the two aspects of something greater than either—the opposing poles of the same Reality. The radical Materialist asserts that the Body is the only reality, and that Mind is merely its "by-product." The Mentalist asserts that the Mind is the only reality, and that the Body is merely its grosser form of manifestation. The unprejudiced philosopher is apt to stand aside and say: "You are both right, yet both wrong—each is stating the truth, but only the half-truth." With the working hypothesis that Mind and Body are but varying aspects of the Truth—that Mind is the inner essence of the Body, and Body the outward manifestation of the Mind—we find ourselves on safe ground.

We mention this fundamental principle here, for in the body of this book we shall not invade the province of metaphysics or philosophy, but shall hold ourselves firmly to our own field, that of psychology. Of course, the very nature of the subject renders it necessary that we consider the influence of psychology upon physiology, but we have remembered that this book belongs to the general subject of the New Psychology, and we have accordingly emphasized the psychological side of the subject. But the same material could have been used by a writer upon physiology, by changing the emphasis from the psychological phase to the physiological.

We have written this book to reach not only those who refuse to see the wonderful influence of the Mental States over the Physical Conditions, but also for our "metaphysical" friends who have become so enamored with the power of the Mind that they practically ignore the existence of the Body, indeed, in some cases, actually denying the existence of the latter. We believe that there is a sane middle-ground in "metaphysical healing," as there is in the material treatment of disease. In this case, not only does Truth lie between the two extremes, but it is composed of the blending and assimilation of the two opposing ideas and theories. But, even if the reader does not fully agree with us in our general theories and conclusions, he will find within the covers of this book a mass of facts which he may use in building up a new theory of his own. And, after all, what are theories but the threads upon which are strung the beads of facts—if our string does not meet with your approval, break it and string the beads of fact upon a thread of your own. Theories come, and theories go—but facts remain.

CHAPTER I

THE SUBCONSCIOUS MIND

In order to understand the nature of the influence of the mind upon the body—the effect of mental states upon physical functions—we must know something of that wonderful field of mental activity which in the New Psychology is known as "The Subconscious Mind," and which by some writers has been styled the "Subjective Mind;" the "Involuntary Mind;" the "Subliminal Mind;" the "Unconscious Mind," etc., the difference in names arising because of the comparative newness of the investigation and classification.

Among the various functions of the Subconscious Mind, one of the most important is that of the charge and control of the involuntary activities and functions of the human body through the agency of the sympathetic nervous system, the cells, and cell-groups. As all students of physiology know, the greater part of the activities of the body are involuntary—that is, are independent (or partly so) of the control of the conscious will. As Dr. Schofield says: "The unconscious mind, in addition to the three qualities which it shares in common with the conscious—*viz.*, will, intellect and emotion—has undoubtedly another very important one—nutrition, or the general maintenance of the body." And as Hudson states: "The subjective mind has absolute control of the functions, conditions and sensations of the body." Notwithstanding the dispute which is still raging concerning *what* the Subconscious mind *is*, the authorities all agree upon the fact that, whatever else it may be, it may be considered as that phase, aspect, part, or field of the mind which has charge and control of the greater part of the physical functioning of the body.

Von Hartmann says: "The explanation that unconscious psychical activity itself appropriately forms and maintains the body has not only nothing to be said against it, but has all possible analogies from the most different departments of physical and animal life in its favor, and appears to be as scientifically certain as is possible in the inferences from effect to cause." Maudsley says: "The connection of mind and body is such that a given state of mind tends to echo itself at once in the body." Carpenter says: "If a psychosis or mental state is produced by a neurosis or material nerve state, as pain by a prick, so also is a neurosis produced by a psychosis. That mental antecedents call forth physical consequents is just as certain as that physical antecedents call forth mental consequents." Tuke says: "Mind, through sensory, motor, vaso-motor and trophic nerves, causes changes in sensation, muscular contraction, nutrition and secretion.... If the brain is an outgrowth from a body corpuscle and is in immediate relation with the structures and tissues that preceded it, then, though these continue to have their own action, the brain must be expected to act upon the muscular tissue, the organic functions and upon the nervous system itself."

Von Hartmann also says: "In willing any conscious act, the unconscious will is evoked to institute means to bring about the effect. Thus, if I will a stronger salivary secretion, the conscious willing of this effect excites the unconscious will to institute the necessary means. Mothers are said to be able to provide through the will a more copious secretion, if the sight of the child arouses in them the will to suckle. There are people who perspire voluntarily. I now possess the power of instantaneously reducing the severest hiccoughs to silence by my own will, while it was formerly a source of great inconvenience to me.... An irritation to cough, which has no mechanical cause, may be permanently suppressed by the will. I believe we might possess a far greater voluntary power over our bodily functions if we were only accustomed from childhood to institute experiments and to practice ourselves therein.... We have arrived at the conclusion that every action of the mind on the body, without exception, is only possible by means of an unconscious will; that such an unconscious will can be called forth partly by means of a conscious will, partly also through the conscious idea of the effect, without conscions will, and even in opposition to the conscious will."

Henry Wood says of the Subconscious Mind: "It acts automatically upon the physical organism. It cognizes external facts, conditions, limitations, and even contagions, quite independent of its active counterpart. One may, therefore, 'take' a disease and be unaware of any exposure. The subconsciousness has been unwittingly trained to fear, and accept it; and it is this quality, rather than the mere inert matter of the body, that succumbs. Matter is never the actor, but is always acted upon. This silent, mental partner, in operation, seems to be a living, thinking personality, conducting affairs on its own account. It is a compound of almost unimaginable variety, including wisdom and foolishness, logic and nonsense, and yet having a working unitary economy. It is a hidden force to be dealt with and educated, for it is often found insubordinate and unruly. It refuses co-operation with its lesser but more active and wiser counterpart. It is very 'set' in its views, and only changes its qualities and opinions by slow degrees. But, like a pair of horses, not until these two mental factors can be trained together can there be harmony and efficiency."

In order to understand the important part played in the physical economy by the Subconscious Mind, it is only necessary to understand the various processes of the human system which are out of the ordinary field of the voluntary or conscious mind. We then realize that the entire process of nutrition, including digestion, assimilation, etc., the processes of elimination, the processes of circulation, the processes of growth, in fact the entire processes manifested in the work of the cells, cell-groups, ganglia, physical organs, etc., are in charge of and controlled by the Subconscious Mind. Our food is digested and transformed into the nourishing substances of the blood; then carried through the arteries to all parts of the body, where it is absorbed by the cells and used to replace the worn-out material, the latter then being carried back through the veins to the lungs where the waste matter is burned up, and the balance again sent on its journey through the arteries re-charged with the life-giving oxygen. All of these processes, and many others of almost equal importance, are out of the field of the conscious or voluntary mind, and are governed by the Subconscious Mind. As we shall see when we consider the Sympathetic Nervous System, the greater part of the body is dominated by the Subconscious Mind, and that the welfare of the major physical functions depends entirely, or almost so, upon this great area or field of the mind.

The best authorities now generally agree that there is no part of the body which may be considered as devoid of mind.

The Subconscious Mind is not confined to the brain, or even the greater plexuses of the nervous system, but extends to all parts of the body, to every nerve, muscle, and even to every cell and cell-group of the body. The functions and processes of the body are no longer considered as purely mechanical, or chemical, but are now seen to be the result of mental action of some kind or degree. Therefore, in considering the Subconscious Mind, one must not think of it as resident in the brain alone, but rather as being *distributed over the entire physical body*. There is mind in every cell, every organ, every muscle, every nerve—in every part of the body.

The importance of the above statements regarding the power and importance of the Subconscious Mind may be realized when one remembers the dictum of the New Psychology, to wit: *The Subconscious Mind is amenable to Suggestion.* When it is realized that this great controller of the physical organism is so constituted that it accepts as truth the suggestions from the conscious mind of its owner, as well as those emanating from the conscious minds of other people, it may be understood why Faith, Belief, and Expectant Attention manifest such marked effects upon the physical body and the general health, for good or for evil, as indicated in the preceding chapters. All of the many instances and examples recited in the preceding chapters may be understood when it is realized that the Subconscious Mind, which is in control of the physical functions and vital processes, will accept the suggestions from the conscious mind of its owner, and also suggestions from outside which the conscious mind of its owner allows to pass down to it. If, as Henry Wood has said in the paragraph previously quoted, it "acts automatically upon the physical organism," and "seems to be a living, thinking personality, conducting affairs on its own account," and at the same time, *accepts and 'takes on' suggested conditions*, it may be readily understood how the wonderful and almost incredible statements of the authorities mentioned in the preceding chapters have had real and substantial basis in truth.

This understanding of the part played by the Subjective Mind in controlling and affecting physical conditions and activities, together with its suggestible qualities and nature, gives us a key to the whole question of the "Why?" of Mental Healing. Suggestion is the connecting link between Mind and Body, and an understanding of its laws and principles enables one to see the moving cause of the strange phenomena of the Faith Cures, under whatever name they may pass, and under whatever guise they may present themselves. "Suggestion" is the explanation offered by the New Psychology for the almost miraculous phenomena which other schools seek to explain upon some hypothesis based either upon religious beliefs, or upon some metaphysical or philosophical doctrine. The New Psychology holds that it is not necessary to go outside of the realms of psychology and physiology in studying Mental Healing or Psycho-Therapy; and that the theories of the semi-religious and metaphysical cults are merely strange guises or masks which serve to conceal the real operative principle of cure.

The following quotation from Dr. Schofield will serve to call the attention to the important part played by the Subconscious Mind in the physical activities, a fact which is not generally recognized: "It has often been a mystery how the body thrives so well with so little oversight or care on the part of its owner. No machine could be constructed, nor could any combination of solids or liquids in organic compounds, regulate, control, counteract, help, hinder or arrange for the continual succession of differing events, foods, surroundings and conditions which are constantly affecting the body. And yet, in the midst of this ever-changing and varying succession of influences, the body holds on its course of growth, health, nutrition and self-maintenance with the most marvelous constancy. We perceive, of course, clearly, that the best of qualities—regulation, control, etc., etc.—are all mental qualities, and at the same time we are equally clear that by no self-examination can we say we consciously exercise any of these mental powers over the organic processes of our bodies. One would think, then, that the conclusion is sufficiently simple and obvious—that they must be used unconsciously; in other words, it is, and can be nothing else than *unconscious mental powers* that control, guide and govern the functions and organs of the body.

"Our ordinary text-books on physiology give but little idea of what I may call the intelligence that presides over the various systems of the body, showing itself in the bones, as we have seen, in distributing the available but insufficient amount of lime salts in disease; not equally, but for the protection of the most vital parts, leaving those of lesser value disproportionally deficient. In the muscular system nearly all contractions are involuntary. Even in the voluntary (so-called) muscles, the most we can do is to will results. We do not will the contractions that carry out these results. Muscles, striped and unstriped, are ceaselessly acting without the slightest consciousness in maintaining the balance of the body, the expression of the face, the general attributes corresponding to mental states, the carrying on of digestion and other processes with a purposiveness, and adaptation of means to new ends and new conditions, ceaselessly arising, that are beyond all material mechanism. Consider, for instance, the marvelous increase of smooth muscle in the uterus at term, and also its no less marvelous subsequent involution; observe, too, the compensating muscular increase of a damaged heart until the balance is restored and the necessity for it ceases, as does growth at a fixed period; consider in detail the repair of a broken bone. These actions are not mere properties of matter; they demand, and are the result of, a controlling mind.

"The circulation does not go round as most text-books would lead us to believe, as the result merely of the action of a system of elastic tubes, connected with a self-acting force-pump. It is such views as these that degrade physiology and obscure the marvels of the body. The circulation never flows for two minutes in the same manner. In an instant, miles of capillaries are closed or opened up, according to the ever-varying body needs, of which, consciously, we are entirely unaware. The blood supply of each organ is not mechanical, but is carefully regulated from minute to minute in health, exactly according to its needs and activities, and when this ever fails, we at once recognize it as disease, and call it congestion and so forth. The very heart-beat itself is never constant, but varies *pro rata* with the amount of exercise, activity of vital functions, of conditions of temperature, etc., and even of emotions and other direct mental feelings. The whole reproductive system is obviously under the sway and guidance of more than blind material forces. In short, when thoroughly analyzed, the action and regulation of no system of the body can be satisfactorily explained, without postulating an unconscious mental element, which *does*, if allowed, satisfactorily explain all the phenomena."

CHAPTER II

THE SYMPATHETIC SYSTEM

The average person has a general understanding of what is meant by "the nervous system," but inquiry will show that by this term he usually includes only that part of the nervous system which is known as the "cerebro-spinal system," or the system of nerves consisting of the brain and spinal cord, and the nerves extending therefrom throughout the body, the offices of which are to control the voluntary movements of the body. The average person is almost entirely ignorant of the existence of the Great Sympathetic System which controls the involuntary movements and processes, such as the processes and functions of nutrition, secretion, reproduction, excretion, the vaso-motor action, etc. In physiology, the term "sympathetic" is used in the sense of: "Reciprocal action of the different parts of the body on each other; an affection of one part of the body in consequence of something taking place in another. Thus when there is a local injury, the whole frame after a time suffers with it. A wound anywhere will tend to create feverishness everywhere; derangement of the stomach will tend to produce headache, liver complaint to produce pain in the shoulder, etc."

An old authority thus describes the Sympathetic Nerves: "A system of nerves, running from the base of the skull to the coccyx, along both sides of the body, and consisting of a series of ganglia along the spinal column by the side of the vertebræ. With this trunk of the sympathetic there are communicating branches which connect the ganglia, or the intermediate cord, with all the spinal and several of the cranial nerves proceeding to primary branches on the neighboring organs or other ganglia, and finally numerous flexures of nerves running to the viscera. Various fibers from the sympathetic communicate with those of the cerebro-spinal system. The term 'sympathetic' has been applied on the supposition that it is the agent in producing sympathy between different parts of the body. It more certainly affects the secretions." In the New Psychology the Sympathetic Nervous System is recognized as that directly under the control of the Subconscious Mind.

The Cerebro-Spinal Nervous System is concerned with the activities arising from the conscious activities of the mind, including those of the five senses. It controls the muscles by which we speak, walk, move our limbs, and pursue the ordinary activities of outer life. But, while these are very important to the individual, there is another set of activities—inner activities—which are none the less important. The Sympathetic System controls the involuntary muscles by means of which the heart throbs, the arteries pulsate, the air is conveyed to the lungs, the blood moves to and from the heart, the various glands and tubes of the body operate, and the entire work of nutrition, repair, and body-building is performed. While the Cerebro-Spinal System, and the Conscious Mind are able to rest a considerable portion of the twenty-four hours of the day, the Sympathetic System and the Subconscious Mind must needs work every minute of the twenty-four hours, without rest or vacation, during the life of their owner.

Dr. E. H. Pratt, in his valuable "Series of Impersonations" published in the medical magazines several years ago, and since reproduced in book form, makes "The Sympathetic Man" speak as follows: "The entire body can do nothing without me; and my occupation of supplying the inspiration for our entire family is so constant and engaging that I am compelled to attend strictly to business night and day from one end of life to the other, and have no time whatever for observation, education, or amusement outside of my daily tasks. As a rule, I perform my work so noiselessly that the rest of the family are scarcely conscious of my existence, for when I am well everything works all right, each organ plays its part as usual, and the entire machinery of life is operated noiselessly and without friction. When I am not well, however, and am not quite equal to the demands made upon me, I have two ways of making it known to the family. One is by appealing to self-consciousness through the assistance of my cerebro-spinal brother, with whom I am closely associated, thereby causing some disturbance of sensation or locomotion (the most frequent disturbance in this direction being the instituting of some form of pain); or I sometimes take it into my head to say nothing to my cerebro-spinal brother about my affairs, but simply shirk my duties, and my inefficiency becomes manifest only when some one or all of the organs suffer from some function poorly performed."

The nerve-centres of the Cerebro-Spinal System are grouped closely together, while those of the Sympathetic System are scattered about the body, each organ having its appropriate centre or tiny-brain. The heart, the liver, the kidneys, the spleen, the brain, the intestinal tract, the bladder, the generative organs, have each its own particular nerve-centre of the Sympathetic System—each its tiny-brain—each, however, connected with all the others. And more than this—in addition to the tiny-brains in each of the important vital organs, there are found scattered through the trunk a number of *ganglia*, or knots of gray nervous matter, arranged longitudinally in two lines extending from just in front of the spinal column from the base of the skull to the end of the spinal column, each vertebra having its appropriate ganglia. In some cases several of these ganglia are grouped together, the number ranging from two to three. Each ganglion is a distinct centre giving off branches in four directions.

There is also one place in which are grouped together several very large ganglia, forming what is known as the Solar Plexus, or Abdominal Brain, which is situated at the upper part of the abdomen, behind the stomach and in front of the aorta and the pillars of the diaphragm, and from which issue nerves extending in all directions. By some authorities the Solar Plexus is regarded as the great centre of the Sympathetic System, and the main seat of the Subconscious Mind. Dr. Byron Robinson bestowed upon this centre the name "The Abdominal Brain," saying of the use of the term: "I mean to convey the idea that it is endowed with the high powers and phenomena of a great nervous centre; that it can organize, multiply, and diminish forces."

One of the most interesting and significant features of the ganglia is that of their connection with the nerve centres of the Cerebro-Spinal System, indicating the reciprocal action existing between the two great nervous systems. From each one of the ganglia in the two great lines forming the system, issues a tiny filament which connects with the spinal cord; and at the same time it receives from the spinal cord a tiny filament in return, thus establishing a double line of communication. It is held by some authorities that one of these filaments acts as a sending wire, and the other as a receiving wire between the two systems. Be this as it may, the inter-communication between the two systems is clearly indicated.

It must be remembered that the involuntary muscles which move the heart, as well as the tiny muscles which form the middle-coat of the arteries and the veins, are controlled by the Sympathetic System, and thus the important work of the circulation, which goes on day and night, year in and year out, during life, is directly under the charge of the Sympathetic System and the Subconscious Mind. Also, the involuntary muscles which are concerned with the activities of the liver, the kidneys and the spleen, are under the same direct control.

Dr. E. H. Pratt, in the "Series of Impersonations" above referred to, makes the "Subconscious Man" tell the following wonderful truth, which we suggest each reader read carefully and fix in his mind: "My brother the Sympathetic Man has told you that I am the animating spirit of his construction; and as he is the great body builder, having furnished the emotions under which our entire family has been put into form, you can understand by what right I pose before you as the human form of forms. All the rest of the family are because I am. Even my Conscious brother, who claims superiority to his fellow-shapes because he bosses them around a little and makes use of them, is a subject of my own creation.... I am the life of the Sympathetic Man, whose existence as a human shape has already sufficiently been well established, and as there is no part of him which is not alive, the conclusion is very evident that his shape and mine are identical. *There is no part of the sympathetic system which is not animated by my own principle of vitality.* Indeed, he is but a cup of life, though I can assure you that his cup is full, and he would not be good for much if it was not. So, if you are able to conceive the shape of the Sympathetic Man, you can regard this form as identical with my own. This is really a very modest claim on my part, and does not quite do justice to myself, for in reality the Sympathetic Man does not contain all there is of me by any means, for I am not only in him, but all around him, and he is not by any means capable of containing my full self."

When it is seen that the vital activities of the physical body are ruled, governed and controlled by the Sympathetic System, animated by the Subconscious Mind, and that the latter is amenable to Suggestion from the Conscious Mind and from outside, we may begin to get a glimmer of the great light which illuminates the principle of Mental Healing. If the Subconscious Mind, *the builder*, is influenced by Suggestion to neglect his work, or to build wrongly, it is likewise possible for him to heed proper Suggestion and to repair his mistakes and to rebuild properly. This principle being grasped, the rest will seem to be merely an understanding of the best methods of reaching the Subconscious Mind by Suggestion or Auto-Suggestion. We may now begin to understand the truth of the old axiom: "As a man thinketh in his heart, so is he"—physically. And as Thought is based largely upon Belief, can we not see the dynamic force of Faith? Is there not a real psychological basis for so-called "miracles?" Is not the wonder-working of the cults now understandable?

CHAPTER III

THE CELL-MINDS

Modern science has demonstrated that the human body is composed of a multitude of microscopic cells, that is, that the muscles, nerves, tissues, blood, bones, hair and nails are made up of minute cells, and groups of cells. Virchow says: "It is of the cells that the tissues are built up and the nerves formed. There is no part of the human body in which the cell is not seen. All these cells are neuclated—have in them a central life-spot like the yolk of an egg. Each cell is born, reproduces itself, dies and is absorbed. The maintenance of life and health depends upon the constant regeneration of the cells. When man can control the life and death of the cell he becomes the creator." Medical science now practically asserts that disease of the body is really disease of the cells of which the body is composed, and that all healing of the body must consist of the healing of the cells—that is, of restoring the cells to normal activity and functioning.

The following quotation from Hudson, following Stephens, is interesting: "An aggregation of cells became a confederation, with its differentiation of cell functions and still further division of labor. As a result of a long process of such differentiation, the organisms of the larger animals and of man came to be composed, as we find them, of thirty or more different species of cells. For example, we have the muscle cells, whose vital energies are devoted to the office of contraction, or vigorous shortening of length; connective-tissue cells, whose office is mainly to produce and conserve a tough fibre for binding together and covering in the organism; bone cells, whose life work is to select and collocate salts of lime for the organic framework, levers and joints; hair, nail, horn and feather cells, which work in silicates for the protection, defense, and ornamentation of the organism; gland cells, whose *motif* in living has come to be the abstraction from the blood of substances which are recombined to produce juices needed to aid the various processes or steps of digestion; blood cells, which have assumed the laborious function of general carriers, scavengers, and repairers of the organism; eye, ear, nasal and palate cells, which have become the special artificers of complicated apparatus for transmitting light, sound, odors, and flavors to the highly sentient brain cells; pulmonary cells, which elaborate a tissue for the introduction of oxygen and the elimination of carbon dioxide and other waste products; hepatic (liver) cells, which have, in response to the needs of the organism, descended to the menial office of living on the waste products and converting them into chemical reagents to facilitate digestion—these and numerous other species of cells; and lastly, most important and of greatest interest, brain and nerve cells."

The various cells of the body are constantly busy, each performing its particular task, either singly or in connection with other cells in the cell-group. Like a great arm, the cells are divided into classes, some being engaged in the active daily work, while others are held back on the reserve line.

Some are engaged in building up the tissues, muscles and bones, while others are busy manufacturing the juices, secretions, fluids and chemical compounds required in the great laboratory of the body. Some remain at their posts, stationary during their entire life, while others remain stationary only until the call comes for their services, while a third class are in constant motion from place to place either following regular routes or else travelling under a roving commission. Some of the moving cells act as carriers of material—the hod-carriers of the body, while others move about doing special repair work such as the healing of wounds, etc., while others still are the scavengers and street cleaners of system, and others form the cell army and cell police force. The body has been compared to a vast communistic or socialistic colony, each member of which cheerfully devotes his life-work, and often his life itself, to the common good. The brain cells are of course the most highly organized, and the most highly differentiated of the cells. The nerve cells constitute a living telegraph system over which is carried the messages from the several parts of the body, each cell being in close contact with its neighbor on each side—the nerve cells practically clasp hands and form a living chain of communication.

The blood cells are important members of the cell-community, and are exceedingly numerous, there being over 75,000,000,000 of the red-blood cells alone. These red-blood cells move in the blood currents, carrying through the arteries each its little load of oxygen which it transports to the distant tissues that they may be invigorated and vitalized anew; and, returning, carrying through the veins the debris and waste products of the system to the great crematory of the lungs where the waste is burnt and thrown off from the body. Like the ships that sail the sea, each cell carries its outgoing cargo, and returns with another one. Some of these cells perform the office of special repairers, forcing their way through the walls of the blood-vessels and penetrating the tissues in order to perform their special tasks. There are several other kinds of cells in the blood besides the carriers just mentioned. There are the wonderful soldier and police cells which maintain order and fight battles when necessary. The police cells are on the constant lookout for germs, bacteria and other microscopic disturbers of the peace of the body. When these tiny policemen discover vagrant germs, or criminal bacteria, they rush upon the intruder and tying him up in a mesh, proceed to devour him. If the intruder be too large or vigorous, a call for assistance is sent out, and the reserve police rush to the assistance of their brothers and overpower the disturber of the peace. Sometimes when the vagrants are too numerous, the policemen throw them out from the body, by means of pimples, boils and similar eruptions. In case of infectious diseases, an army corps is ordered out in full strength and a royal fight is waged between the invading army and the defenders of home and country.

Some of the blood cells take a part in the process of extracting from the food its nourishing particles, and then carrying the same through the blood-channels to all parts of the body, where it is used to feed and nourish the stationary cells there located. These cells manufacture the chemical juices of the body, such as bile, gastric juice, pancreatic juices, milk, etc., in short the entire physical process is carried on by these indefatigable tiny cells. The body of each of us is simply a great community of cells of various kinds. The cells are born by the form of reproduction common to all cells, that of subdivision. Each cell grows until a certain size is reached, when it assumes a "dumb-bell" shape, with a tiny waist line, which waist is afterward dissolved and the two cells move away from each other. In this way, and this way alone, does the body grow, the material required for the enlargement of the cell being supplied from the food and nourishment partaken by the individual. Cells die after having performed their life-work, and their corpses are carried through the veins by the carrier cells, and cast into the crematory of the lungs where they are consumed.

The body is constantly undergoing a process of change and regeneration. Old cells are being cast off every second, and new cells are taking their places. Our muscles, tissues, hair, nails, nerves, brain substance, and even our bones are constantly being made over and rebuilt. Our bodies to-day do not contain a single particle of the material which composed them a few years back. A few weeks suffices to replace our entire skin, and a few months to replace other parts of the body. If a sufficiently large microscope could be placed over our bodies, we would see each part of it as active as a hive of bees, each cell being in action and motion, and the entire domestic work of the human hive being performed according to law and order. Verily, "we are fearfully and wonderfully made."

A number of the best authorities have used the illustration of the process of the cells in healing an ordinary wound, in order to show the activity and "mind" of the tiny cells. We have become so accustomed to the natural healing of a wound, scratch or broken skin, that we have grown to regard it as an almost mechanical process. But, science shows us that there is manifested in the healing process a marvellous degree of life and mind in the cells. Let us consider the process of healing an ordinary wound, that we may see the cells at work. Let us imagine that we are gazing at the wounded part through a marvellously strong microscope which enables us to see every cell at work. If such a glass were provided we should witness a scene similar to that now to be described.

In the first place, through our glass, we should see the gaping wound enlarged to gigantic proportions. We should see the torn skin, tissues, lymphatic and blood vessels, glands, muscles and nerves. We would see the blood pouring forth washing away the dirt and foreign substances that have entered the wound. We would then see the messages calling for help flashing over the living telegraph wires of the nerves, each nerve-cell rapidly passing the word to its neighbor until the great sympathetic centres received the call and sounded the alarm and sent out a "hurry up" call to the cells needed for the repair work. In the meantime the cells of the blood, coming in contact with the outside air have begun to coagulate into a sticky substance, which is the beginning of the scab, the purpose being to close the wound and to hold the severed parts together. The repair cells having now arrived at the scene of the accident begin to mend the break. The tissue, nerve, and muscle cells, on each side of the wound begin to multiply rapidly, receiving their nourishment from the blood cells, and quickly a cell bridge is built up until the two severed edges of the wound are reunited. This bridging is no haphazard process, for the presence of directing law and order is apparent. The newly-born cells of the blood-vessels unite with their brothers on the other side, evenly and in an orderly manner, new tubular channels being formed skillfully. The cells of the connective tissues likewise grow toward each other, and unite in the same orderly manner. The nerve-cells repair their broken lines, just as do a gang of linemen repair the interrupted telegraph system. The muscles are united in the same way. But mark you this, there is no mistake in this connecting process—muscle does not connect with nerve, nor blood-vessel with connective tissue. Finally, the inner repairs and connections having been completed, the scab disappears and the cells of the outer skin rebuild the outer covering, and the wound is healed. This process may occupy a few hours, or many days, depending upon the character of the wound, but the process is the same in all cases. The surgeon merely disinfects and cleans the wound, and placing the parts together allows the cells to perform their healing work, for no other power can perform the task. The knitting together of a broken bone proceeds along the same lines—the surgeon places the parts in juxtaposition, binds the limb together to prevent slipping, and the cells do the rest.

When the body is well nourished, the general system well toned up, and the mind cheerful and active, the repair work proceeds rapidly. But when the physical system is run down, the body poorly nourished, and the mind depressed and full of fear, the work is retarded and interfered with. It is this healing power inherent in the cells that physicians speak of as the *vis vita* or *vis medicatrix naturae*, or "the healing power of nature." Of it Dr. Patton says: "By the term 'efforts of nature' we mean a certain curative or restorative principle, or *vis vita*, implanted in every living or organized body, constantly operative for its repair, preservation and health. This instinctive endeavor to repair the human organism is signally shown in the event of a severed or lost part, as a finger, for instance; for nature unaided will repair and fashion a stump equal to one from the hands of an eminent surgeon.... Nature, unaided, may be equally potent in ordinary illness. Many individuals, even when severely ill, either from motives of economy, prejudice, or skepticism, remain at rest in bed, under favorable hygiene, regimen, etc., and speedily get well without a physician or medicine."

Dr. Schofield says: "The *vis medicatrix naturae* is a very potent factor in the amelioration of disease, if it only be allowed fair play. An exercise of faith, as a rule, suspends the operation of adverse influences, and appeals strongly through the consciousness, to the inner and underlying faculty of vital force (*i. e.*, unconscious mind)." Dr. Bruce says: "We are compelled to acknowledge a power of natural recovery inherent in the body—a similar statement has been made by writers on the principle of medicine in all ages.... The body does possess a means and mechanism for modifying or neutralizing influences which it cannot directly overcome." Oliver Wendell Holmes says: "Whatever other theories we hold we must recognize the '*vis medicatrix naturae*' in some shape or other." Bruce says: "A natural power of the prevention and repair of disorders and disease has as real and as active an existence within us, as have the ordinary functions of the organs themselves." Hippocrates said: "Nature is the physician of diseases." And Ambrose Pare wrote on the walls of the great medical school, the Ecole de Medicine of Paris, these words: "*Je le ponsez et Dieu le guarit*," which translated is: "I dressed the wound, and God healed it."

It is of course true that the life and mind in the cells is derived from the Subconscious Mind, in fact the cells themselves may be said to *embody* the Subconscious Mind, just as the cells of the brain *embody* the Conscious Mind. In every cell there is to be found intelligence in a degree required for the successful performance of the particular task of that cell. Hudson says: "All organic tissue is made up of microscopic cells, each one of which *is a living, intelligent entity*." And, again, "The subordinate intelligences are the cells of which the whole body is composed, *each of which is an intelligent entity, endowed with powers commensurate with its functions*." In short, *the cells of the body are living organs for the expression and manifestation of the Subconscious Mind*. There is not a single cell, group, or part of the party which is devoid of mind. Mind is imminent in the entire body, and in its every part, down to the smallest cell.

The following quotation from Dr. Thomson J. Hudson's "Mental Medicine" clearly expresses a truth conceded by modern science. Dr. Hudson says:

"It follows *a priori*, that every cell in the body is endowed with intelligence; and this is precisely what all biological science tells us is true. Beginning with the lowest form of animal life, the humblest cytode, every living cell is endowed with a wonderful intelligence. There is, in fact, no line to be drawn between life and mind; that is to say, every living organism is a mind organism, from the monera, crawling upon the bed of the ocean, to the most highly differentiated cell in the cerebral cortex of man. Volumes have been written to demonstrate that 'psychological phenomena begin among the very lowest class of beings; they are met with in every form of life, from the simplest cellule to the most complicated organism. It is they that are the essential phenomena of life, inherent in all protoplasm.' (Binet.) It is, in fact, an axiom of science that the lowest unicellular organism is endowed with the potentialities of manhood. I have remarked that each living cell is endowed with a wonderful intelligence. This is emphatically true, whether it is a unicellular organism or a constituent element of a multicellular organism. Its wonderful character consists not so much in the amount of intelligence possessed by each individual cell, as it does in the quality of that intelligence. That is to say, each cell is endowed with an instinctive, or intuitive, knowledge of all that is essential to the preservation of its own life, the conservation of its energies, and the perpetuation of its species. In other words, it is endowed with an intuitive knowledge of the laws of its own being, which knowledge is proportioned to its stage of development and adapted to its environment."

The cell has the intelligence sufficient to enable it to seek nourishment, and to move from one place to another in search for food or for other purposes. It holds to its food when secured, and envelops it until it is absorbed and digested. It exercises the power of choice, accepting and selecting one portion of food in preference to another. It has the power of discriminating between nourishing food and the reverse. The authorities show that it has a rudimentary memory, and avoids the repetition of an unpleasant or painful experience, and also returns to the locality in which it has previously secured food. Biological experiments have shown that the cells are capable of experiencing surprise, pleasure and fear, and that they experience different degrees of feeling, and react accordingly in response to stimuli. Verworn, a biologist, even goes so far as to assert that they habitually adapt means to ends, near and remote. In his remarkable work on cell-life, "The Psychic Life of Micro-organisms," Binet says: "We shall not regard it as strange, perhaps, to find so complete a psychology in the history of the lower organisms, when we call to mind that, agreeably to the ideas of evolution now accepted, a higher animal is nothing more than a colony of protozoans. Every one of the cells composing such an animal has retained its primitive properties, giving them a higher degree of perfection by division of labor and by selection. The epithelial cells that secrete the nails and hair are organisms perfected with reference to the secretion of protective parts. Similarly, the cells of the brain are organisms that have been perfected with reference to psychical attributes."

Dr. Schofield says: "That life involves mind has, of course, like all else, been vigorously disputed and equally vigorously affirmed. 'Life,' says Prof. Bascom, 'is not force; it is combining power. *It is the product and presence of mind.*' ... The extent to which the word mind may be employed as the inherent cause of purposive movements in organisms is a very difficult question to solve. There can be no doubt that the actual agents in such movements are the natural forces, but behind these the directing and starting power seems to be psychic.... There being an indwelling power, not only for purposive action in each cell, but for endless combinations of cell activities for common ends not at all connected with the mere nutrition of the single cell, but for the good of the completed organism." Dr. R. Dunn says: "From the first movement when the primordial cell-germ of a human organism comes into being, the entire individual is present, fitted for human destiny. From the same moment, matter, life and mind are never for an instant separated, their union constituting the essential work of our present existence." Carpenter says: "The convertibility of physical forces and correlation of these with the vital and the intricacy of that nexus between mental and bodily activity which cannot be analyzed, all lead upwards towards one and the same conclusion—*the source of all power is mind.* And that physical conclusion is the apex of the pyramid which has its foundation in the primitive instincts of humanity."

Having seen the evidences of life and mind in the single cell, let us now proceed to a consideration of the intelligence or mind inherent and manifest in the groups of cells, large and small, including the largest groups which compose the several organs of the body. This line of investigation will lead us to a fuller understanding of the influence of the mental states upon the health or disease of the organs and parts. It will be seen that Mental Healing has a sound biological as well as a psychological basis of truth, and that it is not necessary to invade the fields of metaphysics or theology in order to find an explanation of the effect of mind over body.

CHAPTER IV

THE MENTAL BASIS OF CURE

We have seen that in each cell in the human body is embodied a part of the Subconscious Mind, sufficient in quantity and quality to enable the cell to perform its particular work in the physical community of cells. In the same manner each group of cells, large or small, is possessed of the quantity and quality of mind adapted to the successful performance of its particular function. And, rising in the scale, we find that each of the physical organs is possessed of a "composite cell-soul" or "organ-mind." As Hudson says: "Each organ of the body is composed of a group of cells which are differentiated with special reference to the functions to be performed by that organ. In other words, every function of life is performed by groups of co-operative cells, so that the body as a whole is simply a confederation of the various groups."

For instance, as Haeckel says: "This 'tissue soul' is the higher psychological function which gives physiological individuality to the compound multicellular organism as a true 'cell commonwealth.' It controls all the separate 'cell souls' of the social cells—the mutually dependent 'citizens' which constitute the community.... The human egg-cell, as soon as it is fertilized, multiplies by division and forms a community, or colony of many social cells. These differentiate themselves, and by their specialization, by various modifications of these cells, the various tissues which compose the various organs are developed. The developed many-celled organisms of man and of all higher animals resemble, therefore, a social civil community, the numerous single individuals of which are, indeed, developed in various ways, but which were originally only simple cells of one common structure."

Biology shows us that there are unquestionably methods of communication between cell and cell, although it has not as yet been definitely determined just how this communication is effected. In the cell-communities of the micro-organisms there is undoubtedly present the power to communicate on the part of the several cells composing the community, and the pain or discomfort of one part is evidently felt by the whole community. Just as an army, or a congregation, has a mind common to the whole, in addition to the individual minds of its units, so has every organ of the body an "organ mind" in addition to the individual cell minds of its unit cells. The fact of the existence of "group-mind," or "collective-mind" is recognized by the best authorities in modern psychology, and the study of its principles throws light on some hitherto perplexing phenomena.

Prof. Le Bon, in his work "The Crowd," says of the "collective mind" of men: "The sentiments and ideas of all the persons in the gathering take one and the same direction, and their conscious personality vanishes. A collective mind is formed, doubtless transitory, but presenting very clearly marked characteristics. The gathering has become what, in the absence of a better expression, I will call an organized crowd, or, if the term be considered preferable, a psychological crowd. *It forms a single being,* and is subjected to the law of the mental unity of crowds.... The most striking peculiarity presented by a psychological crowd is the following: Whoever be the individuals that compose it, however like or unlike be their mode of life, their occupation, their character, or their intelligence, the fact that they have been transformed into a crowd puts them in possession of *a sort of collective mind,* which makes them feel, think, and act in a manner quite different from that in which each individual of them would feel, think and act, were he in a state of isolation. There are certain ideas and feelings which do not come into being, or do not transform themselves into acts, except in the case of the individuals forming a crowd.... In the collective mind the intellectual aptitudes of the individuals, and in consequence their individuality, is weakened.... The most careful observations seem to prove that an individual immerged for some length of time in a crowd in action soon finds itself in a special state, which most resembles the state of fascination in which the hypnotized individual finds himself.... The conscious personality has entirely vanished, will and discernment are lost. All feelings and thoughts are bent in the direction determined by the hypnotizer.... An individual in a crowd is a grain of sand amid other grains of sand, which the wind stirs up at will."

In short, psychology recognizes a *mental fusion* between the individual minds of units composing a community of cells, insects, higher animals and even men. The "spirit of the hive" noted by all students of bee-life, and the community spirit in an ant-hill are instances serving to illustrate the general principle of "the collective mind." As we have seen in the preceding chapter, the entire human body is a vast community of cells, each unit in the community having relations with every other unit, and all having sprung from the same original egg-cell. This great community, or *nation* of cells is divided into many smaller communities, chief among which are the principal organs of the body, as the stomach, the intestines, the liver, the kidneys, the spleen, the heart, etc. And, following the general rule, each of these organ-communities possesses its own "collective mind," subordinate, of course, to the great community mind known as the Subconscious Mind. Ordinarily these communities live in peace and harmony, and in obedience to the national government. But occasionally rebellions and revolutions are started, which cause much inharmony, pain and disease. Sometimes these rebellions arise from abuse of the particular organ by its owner, or from sympathy with another abused organ, or from general abuse of the system. But, at other times, there seems to be an active discontent springing up in an organ, to the quelling of which the entire Subconscious Mind bends its energy and forces. Very often these rebellions are started by adverse auto-suggestions or fearthoughts emanating from the conscious mind of the individual, which act according to the law of suggestion and practically *hypnotize* the mind of the organ in question.

This idea of each organ having a mind of its own—being practically an entity, in fact—may be somewhat startling to those who have never had the matter presented to them, but the statement is backed up by the best scientific authorities who, however, do not usually state it in so plain terms, or popular form. It is likely that the science of the future will make some great discoveries regarding this matter of the "collective mind" of the organs, and that the schools of medicine will adapt the new knowledge to the treatment of disease. In the meantime, the practitioners of Mental Healing are availing themselves of this principle, often without realizing the principle itself.

The writer has been interested in this subject of the "organ mind" for a number of years, and has conducted a number of experiments along this line, the result being that he feels more firmly convinced each year of the truth of the theory or idea. He has found that mental treatments based on this theory have been very successful, much more so in fact than those conducted in pursuance to other theories. It seems that by applying the suggestive treatment direct to the affected organ a quicker response is had. The writer is indebted to Dr. Paul Edwards, a well known mental healer, who several years ago advanced the idea that the mind or "intelligence" in the several organs differed greatly in temperament and quality. He informed us that he had proven to his own satisfaction that the heart is "*very* intelligent," and quite amenable to mild, gentle, coaxing suggestions, advice or orders; while, on the other hand, the liver is a most mulish, stubborn, obstinate organ-mind, which requires one to drive it in a sharp positive manner. Investigation along these lines suggested by Dr. Edwards has convinced the writer that the theory is warranted by the facts. Experiments have shown that the heart organ-mind is gentle, mild, and easily influenced by kindly suggestion, advice and requests, and that it needs but a word directed to it to attract its attention. Likewise, the liver has been found to be brutish, stubborn and obstinate, needing the most vigorous suggestions—in short the liver-mind is a donkey and must be so treated. The liver-mind is sluggish, torpid and sleepy, and needs much prodding before it will "sit up and take notice." The stomach has been found to be quite intelligent, especially when it has not been brutalized by "stuffing." It will readily respond to suggestive treatment of all kinds, it being noticed that it may be easily flattered or "jollied" into good behavior, just as may certain children. The nervous system has a mind of its own, and will accept suggestions, although it is usually difficult to attract its attention, owing to its habit of concentration upon its regular work. The bowel-mind will respond to firm, kind treatment, as will also the uterus-mind and the mind controlling the other organs peculiar to women.

In another work, the writer has said regarding this form of treatment of the organs through their organ-minds: "Remember, always, that you are mind talking to mind, not to dead matter. There is mind in every cell, nerve, organ and part of the body, and in the body as a whole, and this mind will listen to your central mind and obey it, because your central mind is positive to it—the organ is negative to *you*. Carry this idea with you in giving these treatments, and endeavor to visualize the mind in the organs, as clearly as may be, for by so doing you get them in better *rapport* with you, and can handle them to better advantage. And always remember that the virtue lies not in the mere sound of the words that happen to reach the organ or cells—they do not understand words as words, but they do understand the meaning behind the words. But without words it is very hard for you to think, or clearly express the feeling—and so, by all means use the words just as if the organ-mind understood the actual meaning thereof, for by so doing you can drive in the meaning of the word—and induce the mental state and conditions necessary to work the cure.

Dr. S. F. Meacham, in a magazine article published several years ago, said: "Let me once more call your attention to that one great principle of disease and cure. It is the only medical creed I hold to-day and will bear repeating, lest we neglect it. *Disease is a failure of the cells to make good their waste, or to do their full duty*. This may be an individual matter with the cell, or may result from imperfect co-operation; there may be a mutiny in the co-operative commonwealth constituting the body. Apart from all mutual help, or co-operation of cells, each individual cell must either do its full duty, or suffer, and perchance die, as the result. Remember that each individual cell lives, and has an office that no other cell can fill to save it. If the other cell does the work, it will live, but the failing cell will not profit thereby. By co-operating they may lighten each other's labors, but *no cell is or can be exempt from doing its part.* Any failure of this kind is disease either local or general, according to the degree and nature of the failure, or according to the importance of the mutinous or weakened cell. A cure results when the cells again do their work. Or, if a certain number die, a cure is established when other cells learn to do that particular work, which is sometimes the case. A remedy is any substance, or force, or procedure that will stimulate, or help, or remove obstacles that prevent these cells from doing their work. *Keep in mind, that the life process acting through or in the cell does the work either aided, or alone.* The lesson then is that all these methods do good, and that owing to the view point, mental status, or expectancy of the individual, now one and now another method will appeal to him and be accepted. No matter what we do, we aid, we assist only—we do not cure.... *The process going on in each cell is an intelligent one,* and all extrinsic methods are really but suggestions offered to the cell, the real worker; and the fact is that any one of these helps may be chosen, and all may be rejected...."

"The repair of a cell is as equally as intellectual a process as any other can be. If, for instance, blind force can repair one cell, it can many; if it can build one, it can all, and mind and intellect are then without causal efficacy, without spontaneity, and blind force, fatality and purposeless action reign supreme.... According to this theory the building and repairing of cells would not be intellectual, as there would be no working plan or purpose. I am aware that a purely extrinsic study of the cells and of the body will force this conclusion upon any candid, unprejudiced mind; but *a study from the inside* is a different matter. A cell, looked at from without, moves only when stimulated; but is this really true? The body is but a compound of cells when viewed from the outside; then if one cell moves when stimulated, why not twenty, a hundred, a thousand, a billion, the entire body? But is it true of the body? You come to me and propose some scheme, or act, which I carry out. Now is your proposition the real cause of my act, or only a condition? Do I not choose, and either do the thing or not, as determined from within? If this is true of the body, why not of the cell? May not the stimulation we see be a condition only, and the real cause of the act be within the cell itself?... The cell is not a mere machine, *but a living entity*, doing everything that the body does. It eats, drinks, moves, reproduces its kind, selects its food, repairs its waste, etc. These are intellectual processes, but may not be conscious....

"The cure consists in the repairing of the wasted tissue, and in the cells restoring and repairing themselves into a definite pattern, necessary to mutual work, so that the commonwealth may prosper. Air, water, sunshine, food, etc., are necessary to the performance of this work of repair. When these are furnished, even under the best conditions possible, the cells must use them to build up the waste, and this they do by their internal forces. But this process is what is called repair on the one hand, and cure on the other. External means may be essential, but that will not make them really curative.... It is well, also, to keep in mind that external in the true sense of the term as we are using it here. *Any force outside of the diseased cell is an external force to that cell even if it be thought-force.* Disease is always treated by external force, external as defined above, and all disease is just as surely cured by internal force—viz.: *force resident in the cell itself.* Here we all stand around the suffering cell, one with drug-power in his hand, another with electricity, or water, or heat, or directed attention—thought-force or more nourishment which necessitates a better circulation to that area, or some other of the thousand therapeutic measures, and we are close enough together at last to see that we are simply using different stimuli to try to aid the real worker within the cell to do his work by furnishing, not only material that is necessary, but force as well, that out of the abundance his work may be easy and rapid."

The reader who will consider the numerous instances of cure by Suggestion or Faith-Cure, as noted in the following chapters, will be better able to understand the principle underlying these cures if he will realize the fact brought out so forcibly by Dr. Meacham, as above quoted. The attention of the patient being directed to the organ affected, in connection with the stimulating and vitalizing effect of Faith and Belief, starts into renewed activity the cell-mind of the organ in question, and arouses its reparative and recuperative energies. Each organ, and its component cells and cell-groups, is of course under the control of the Subconscious Mind, and forms a part of the material embodiment thereof. The Subconscious Mind, being stimulated by the Suggestion and Faith, and having its Expectant Attention aroused, concentrates its energies upon the reparative and recuperative processes in the organ, and the work of cure proceeds. The cure, in every case, is simply either repair work, or else the restoration of normal functioning—in either case the cells themselves doing the work.

In the consideration of the reasons underlying the cure of disease by Psycho-Therapeutics, we must first consider the question of what disease really is. And in this phase of the consideration, it will be well for us to first dispel the erroneous ideas concerning disease which we have been entertaining. Perhaps the following striking statement from Sidney

Murphy, M. D., printed in the magazine "Suggestion" several years ago, may help you to form a correct idea of the nature of disease, or rather a correct idea of what disease *is not*. Dr. Murphy says, in the said article, among other things: "Prof. S. D. Gross, formerly of the New York University Medical School, says: 'Of the essence of disease very little is known—indeed nothing at all.' Nevertheless it is evident that medical men have an idea on the subject. The theory generally held, I believe, is that disease is destructive action; but just what this means, whether destructive action on the part of vitality itself, or by something acting upon the vitality, is not so clear; but we are enabled to gain some light by reference to the expression used in medical books concerning it. Thus we find that disease 'attacks us,' that it 'seats itself in an organ,' that 'it works through us, runs its course,' etc. It is also said to be 'very malignant,' or 'quite mild,' 'persistently resisting all treatment,' or 'yielding readily' to it. In fact, it is considered an entity, possessing character and disposition and general vital qualities—a something which domiciles itself in the vital domain, and exercises its forces to the destruction of the vital powers. It is indeed spoken of as one would speak of a rat in his granary, or a mouse in his cupboard, and efforts are made to dislodge it, or kill it, as one would dislodge or kill any other living thing. This theory of disease is beginning to be looked upon even by the medical world as untenable. Living things are always possessed of organizations having form or shape; and hence if disease were such, its form would be discerned and described; a thing which never has been done. Disease by our ancestors was considered a subtile and mysterious thing which pounced down upon us, and runs its course without any reference to causes; and language being formed to convey this idea, it has been transmitted almost unchanged from generation to generation down to the present time. And the medical profession of to-day is simply an embodiment of that idea. It is probable that the term 'destructive action' is generally held to mean destructive action on the part of the vitality itself.... Life in organic form is developed according to law. Slowly rising into power, organization at length reaches its zenith, and then goes down the gentle declivity, until the soul steps off into the great beyond, without pain or struggle, provided always that the conditions of life are natural and therefore favorable; but if these be unfavorable, unfavorable results must of course follow; vitality, nevertheless, doing the best it can under the circumstances to preserve the normal state of the body. Disease, we propose to show, is not antagonistic to vital action, but the opposite, a remedial effort, *or vital action on the defensive.* It is not a downward tendency, nor the result of a downward tendency on the part of a living organism, but is itself an upward or self-preservative tendency, the result of disobedience to natural laws. *It is simply abnormal action, because of abnormal conditions.*"

In considering the above revolutionary statement of Dr. Murphy, we must remember that "vitality" or "vital force" is simply the action of the Subconscious Mind operating through the sympathetic system, the organ-minds, and the cell-minds. *All vital energy, at the last is mental energy.* And, we must also remember that the "abnormal conditions" which Dr. Murphy speaks of as being the cause of "abnormal action" or disease, are not confined alone to physical or material conditions, but also to abnormal mental conditions, such as fear-thought, adverse suggestions, improper use of the imagination, etc. As we have seen in the preceding chapters, the causes of disease may be mental as well as material or physical.

The Subconscious Mind in its vital activities is constantly at work building up, repairing, growing, nourishing, supporting and regulating the body, doing its best to throw off abnormal conditions, and seeking to do the best it can when these conditions cannot be removed. With its source pure and unpolluted the stream of vitality flows on unhindered, but when the poison of fear-thought, adverse suggestion and false belief is poured into the source or spring from which the stream rises, it follows that the waters of life will no longer be pure and clear. Let us notice the general direction of the vital activities of the Subconscious Mind.

In the first place we find that the vital activities are primarily concerned with *self-preservation*, that is with the preservation of the individual and the race. One has but to notice the ever-present manifestation of the "race instinct" which draws the males and females of the several species together, that they may mate and bring forth the young needed to keep alive the species. The parental devotions, with its many sacrifices of personal pleasure for the young, are instances ever before us. And no less striking is the companion activities which make for the preservation of the individual. The instinctive tendency toward self-preservation is so strong that it overpowers the reason in the majority of cases. Men may decry the value of life, but let their life be threatened and the instinctive protective feeling causes them to fight for life against all odds. "All that a man hath will he give for his life." And this instinctive activity is manifest not only in the individual as a whole, but in every cell of his body. Every cell is striving hard for the welfare of the community of which it forms a part. Even in disease it strives to throw off the abnormal conditions which afflict the body, and failing to do so it hobbles along doing the best it can under the circumstances.

The tiny seed sprouting in the ground, and lifting weights a thousand times that of itself, shows the self-preservative energies and activities of the mind principle within it. The healing work of the cells in the case of a wound, or of a broken bone, as described elsewhere in this book, gives us another example. The healing efforts of the organism striving to throw off the morbid substances within the body, purging them away in a flux, or burning them up with a fever, show the operations of the same principle. This, we have seen, is called the *vis medicatrix naturae*, or "healing power of nature," which operates in man as well as in the case of the lower animals—but it is really but the operations of the great Subconscious Mind of the individual. As Dr. Murphy, previously quoted, says: "Certainly all experience declares and all physicians will admit that where vital power is abundant in a man he will get well from almost any injuries short of complete destruction of vital organs; but where vitality is low, recovery is much more difficult, if not impossible, which can only be explained on the principle that vitality always works upward toward life and health to the extent of its ability under the circumstances, because, if it worked downward, the less vitality, the more surely and speedily would death result."

Following the law of self-preservation, we find that of *accommodation* manifesting itself in the vital activities of the Subconscious Mind. This principle or law works in the direction of *adjusting the organism to conditions which it cannot remedy*. Thus a sapling bent out of shape, will bend its branches upward until once more they will reach toward the sky notwithstanding the deformed trunk. Seed sprouting from a narrow crevice in a rock, and unable to split the rock, will assume a deformed shape but will hold tenaciously to life, and will thrive under these abnormal conditions. This principle of accommodation acts upon the idea of "life at any price," and of "making the best of things." Man and the lower animals accommodate themselves to their environment, when they are unable to overcome the unsatisfactory conditions of the latter. The study of anthropology, natural history, and botany will convince anyone that the principle of accommodation is everywhere present in connection with that of self-preservation. And the diseased conditions, and abnormal functioning, which we find in cases of chronic diseases is simply the principle of accommodation in the vital activities of the Subconscious Mind, but which it is "trying to make the best of it," and holding on to "life at any price."

Dr. Murphy, previously quoted, says: "Disease, in its essential nature, has a deeper significance than simply abnormal manifestations. It is really a remedial effort, not necessarily successful, but an attempt to change, or have changed existing conditions. And for this reason any improper relation of the living organism to external agents necessarily results in an injury to that organism, which by virtue of its being self-preservative, immediately sets up defensive action, and begins as soon as possible to repair the damages that have accrued. This defensive or reparative action, of course, corresponds to the conditions to be corrected, and hence is abnormal and diseased; and its severity and persistence will depend upon the damages to be repaired, and the intensity and persistence of the causes that produced it. Serious injury present or impending will demand serious vital action; desperate conditions, desperate action. But in all cases the action is vital, an attempt at restoration, and the energy displayed will exactly correspond to the interests involved and the vitality that is available."

From the above, and from what has been shown in previous chapters, it will be seen that just as is health the result of the normal functioning of the Subconscious Mind, so is disease the result of its abnormal functioning. And it may also be seen that the true healing power must come alone from and through the Subconscious Mind itself, although the same may be aroused, awakened and directed by various outside agencies. As Dr. Thomson J. Hudson says: "Granted that there is an intelligence that controls the functions of the body in health, it follows that it is the same power or energy that fails in case of disease. Failing, it requires assistance; and that is what all therapeutic agencies aim to accomplish. No intelligent physician of any school claims to be able to do more than to 'assist nature' to restore normal conditions of the body. That it is a mental energy that thus requires assistance, no one denies; for science teaches us that the whole body is made up of a confederation of intelligent entities, each of which performs its functions with an intelligence exactly adapted to the performance of its special duties as a member of the confederacy. There is, indeed, no life without mind, from the lowest unicellular organism up to man. *It is therefore a mental energy that actuates every fiber of the body under all its conditions. That there is a central intelligence that controls each of these mind organisms, is self-evident....* It is sufficient for us to know that such an intelligence exists, and that, for the time being, it is the controlling energy that normally regulates the action of the myriad cells of which the body is composed. *It is, then, a mental organism that all therapeutic agencies are designed to energize, when, for any cause, it fails to perform its functions with reference to any part of the physical structure."*

CHAPTER V

THE HISTORY OF PSYCHO-THERAPY

One of the most remarkable achievements of the New Psychology is that of gathering up the scattered instances of the effect of the power of the mind over the body, under the various masks and guises worn during the ages, and uniting them in one broad and general synthesis in which is to be seen the one fundamental principle of Mental Healing operating under a thousand names, forms and theories, in every race, nation and clime in all ages past and present. The New Psychology is the great reconciler of the various theories, dogmas and speculations concerned with the subject of the strange cures effected by the mind, as well as with the equally strange adverse effect upon the physical organism of negative thoughts.

From the earliest days of history we find records of strange and marvelous cures effected by non-material agents. In some cases the effect is attributed to magical power, while in others, and the majority of cases, the cure is attributed to some particular religious belief, creed or ceremony. Not only in the folk-lore of the several races, and in their general traditions, but also in the written and graven record do we find traces of the universality of the principle of mental therapeutics.

H. Addington Bruce says: "Psychotherapy might well be cited in support of the old adage that there is nothing new but what has been forgotten. Traces of it are to be found almost as far back as authentic history extends, and even allusion to methods which bear a strong resemblance to those of modern times. The literature and monumental remains of ancient Egypt, Greece, Rome, Persia, India and China reveal a widespread knowledge of hypnotism and its therapeutic value. There is in the British Museum a bas-relief from Thebes which has been interpreted as representing a physician hypnotizing a patient by making 'passes' over him. According to the Ebers papyrus, the 'laying on of hands' formed a prominent feature of Egyptian medical practice as early as 1552 B. C., or nearly thirty-five hundred years ago; and it is known that a similar mode of treatment was employed by priests of Chaldea in ministering to the sick. So, also, the priests of the famous Temples of Health are credited with having worked numerous cures by the mere touch of the hands. In connection with these same Temples of Health were sleeping chambers, repose in which was supposed to be exceptionally beneficial. Asclepiades of Bithynia, who won considerable fame at Rome as a physician, systematically made use of the 'induced trance' in the treatment of certain diseases. Plautus, Martial, and Seneca refer in their writings to some mysterious process of manipulation which had the same effect—that is, of putting persons into an artificial sleep. And Solon sang, apparently, of some form of mesmeric cure:

"'The smallest hurts sometimes increase and rage
More than all art of physic can assuage;

Sometimes the fury of the worst disease
The hand by gentle stroking, will appease.'

"Many other instances might be mentioned testifying to the remarkable extent to which psycho-therapy, in one form or another, was utilized in the countries of the ancient world. This, of course, does not necessarily imply that the ancients had any real understanding of the psychological and physiological principles governing its operation. On the contrary, there is every reason to believe that they used it much as do too many of the mental healers of to-day—on the basis of 'faith cure' pure and simple, with no attempt at diagnosis, and in a hit-or-miss fashion. It was not until the very end of the Middle Ages, so far as history informs us, that anything even remotely resembling a scientific inquiry into its nature and possibilities was undertaken, and then only in a faint, vague, indefinite way, by men who were metaphysicians and mystics rather than scientists. The first of these, Petrys Pomponatius, a sixteenth-century philosopher, sought to prove that disease was curable without drugs, by means of the 'magnetism' existing in certain specially gifted individuals. 'When those who are endowed with this faculty,' he affirmed, 'operate by employing the force of the imagination and the will, this force affects their blood and their spirits, which produce the intended effects by means of an evaporation thrown outwards.' Following Pomponatius, John Baptist von Helmont, to whom medical science owes a great deal, also proclaimed the curative virtue of magnetism, which he described as an invisible fluid called forth and directed by the influence of the human will. Other writers, notably Sir Kenelm Digby, laid stress on the power of the imagination as an agent in the cause as well as the cure of disease, compiling in a curious little treatise published in 1658, as interesting a collection of illustrative cases as is contained in the literature of modern psycho-therapy."

In the Middle Ages, we read that there were many instances of miraculous cures effected at the various shrines of the saints, and in the churches in which were exhibited the bones and other relics of the holy people of church history. As Dr. George R. Patton says: "A word scrawled upon parchment, for instance, would cure fevers; an hexameter from the Iliad of Homer cured gout, while rheumatism succumbed to a verse from Lamentations. These could be multiplied, and undoubtedly all were equally potent of cure in like manner.... At one time holy wells were to be found in almost every parish of Ireland, to which wearisome journeys were made for the miraculous powers of cure. It was the custom of the cured to hang upon the bushes contiguous to the springs small fragments of their clothing, or a cane, or a crutch as a memento of cure, so that from afar the springs could be easily located by the many colored fragments of clothing, rags, canes and crutches swayed upon the branches by the wind. Inasmuch as the bushes for many rods around were thus adorned, the cures must have been far from few."

In the Middle Ages it was the custom of persons afflicted with scrofula and kindred disorders to come before the king upon certain days to receive the "Royal Touch," or laying-on-of-hands which was held to be an infallible specific for the disease. The custom was instituted by Edward the Confessor, and continued until the accession to power of the house of Brunswick. It is a matter of history that many persons were cured by the touch of the king's hands. Wiseman, a celebrated surgeon and physician of old London testifies as follows: "I myself have been an eye-witness of many thousands of cures performed by his majesty's touch alone, without any assistance of medicine or surgery, and those, many of them, such as had tired out the endeavors of able surgeons before they came hither.... I must needs profess that what I write will little more than show the weakness of our ability when compared with his majesty's, who cureth more in one year than all the surgeons of London have done in an age." The virtue of the "King's Touch" was finally brought in doubt by the wonderful successes of a man by the name of Valentine Greatrakes, who in the Seventeenth Century began "laying on hands" and made even more wonderful cures than those of the king. So marked was his success that the government had difficulty in suppressing the growing conviction among the common people that Greatrakes must be of royal blood, and the rightful heir to the throne, because of the great healing virtues of his hands, which, they argued, could be possessed only by those having royal blood in their veins. The Chirurgical Society of London investigated Greatrakes' cures, and rendered an opinion that he healed by virtue of "some mysterious sanative contagion in his body."

But perhaps the most notable figure in the European history of Mental Healing was Franz Anton Mesmer, a native of Switzerland, who was born in 1734, and who later in the century created the greatest excitement in several European countries by his strange theories and miraculous claims. Frank Podmore in a recent work says of Mesmer: "He had no pretensions to be a thinker; he stole his philosophy ready-made from a few belated alchemists; and his entire system of healing was based on a delusion. His extraordinary success was due to the lucky accident of the times. Mesmer's first claim to our remembrance lies in this—that he wrested the privilege of healing from the churches and gave it to mankind as a universal possession."

Mesmer held that there was in Nature a universal magnetic force which had a powerful therapeutic effect when properly applied. He cured many people by touching them with an iron rod, through which he claimed the universal magnetism flowed from his body to that of the patient. He called this magnetic fluid "animal magnetism." Later on he devised his celebrated "magnetic tub" or *baquet*, by means of which he was able to treat his patients *en masse*. Podmore gives the following interesting account of scenes surrounding his treatments:

"The baquet was a large oaken tub, four or five feet in diameter and a foot or more in depth, closed by a wooden cover. Inside the tub were placed bottles full of water disposed in rows radiating from the center, the necks in some of the rows pointing towards the center, in others away from it. All these bottles had been previously 'magnetized' by Mesmer. Sometimes there were several rows of bottles, one above the other; the machine was then said to be at high pressure. The bottles rested on layers of powdered glass and iron filings. The tub itself was filled with water. The whole machine, it will be seen, was a kind of travesty of the galvanic cell. To carry out the resemblance, the cover of the tub was pierced with holes, through which passed slender iron rods of varying lengths, which were jointed and movable, so that they could be readily applied to any part of the patient's body. Round this battery the patients were seated in a circle, each with his iron rod. Further, a cord, attached at one end to the tub, was passed round the body of each of the sitters, so as to bind them all into a chain. Outside the first a second circle would frequently be formed, who would connect themselves together by holding hands. Mesmer, in a lilac robe, and his assistant operators—vigorous and handsome young men selected for the purpose—walked about the room, pointing their fingers or an iron rod held in their hands at the diseased parts."

Mesmer made many wonderful cures, and attracted wide attention. In 1781 the king of France offered him a pension of thirty thousand livres if he would make public his secret. The offer was refused, but he gave private instruction and opened a school. He had many pupils and followers, prominent among whom was the Marquis de Puysegur, who made discoveries resulting in the identification of Mesmerism with the "trance condition" now commonly associated with the term, whereas originally Mesmerism included simply the healing process. Mesmer's methods continued popular for many years after his death, until Braid's work resulted in the founding of the modern school of Hypnotism, and Mesmerism died out.

The Abbe Faria, about 1815, after investigating Mesmerism and attracting much attention, discarded the "fluidic" theory of Mesmer, and held, instead, that in order to induce the mesmeric state and to produce the phenomena thereof, it was necessary merely to create a mental state of "expectant attention" on the part of the patient. The cause of the state and the phenomena, he held, was not in the operator but in the mind of the patient—purely subjective, in fact. Alexander Bertrand, a Frenchman, published a work about this time, holding theories similar to those of Faria. In 1841 James Braid, an English physician, becoming interested in Mesmerism, discovered that the mesmeric state might be artificially induced by staring at bright objects until the eyes became fatigued, etc., and, later, that any method whereby concentration and "expectant attention" might be induced would produce the phenomenon. He duplicated all the feats of the mesmerists, including the healing of diseases. He called his new system "Hypnotism" to distinguish it from Mesmerism, and under its new name it gained favor among the medical fraternity. Moreover, in connection with his predecessors, Faria and Bertrand, he laid the basis for the modern theories of Suggestive Therapeutics.

Shortly after Braid's death, in 1860, Dr. A. A. Liebault, a French physician, established his since famous School of Nancy, in which during the after years the later wonderful discoveries in Suggestive Therapeutics were made. He used the methods of hypnotism, but Suggestion was ever the operative principle recognized and applied. Liebault said: "It is all a matter of Suggestion. My patients are *suggested* to sleep, and their ills are *suggested* out of them. It is very simple, once you understand the laws of Suggestion." Dr. Charcot, in his celebrated clinic in the Salpetriere, in Paris, did great work along the same general lines, although proceeding under somewhat different theories. Following the example of these and other eminent authorities, the medical fraternity has gradually adopted many of the ideas of Suggestive Therapeutics, and today many of the best medical schools throughout this country and Europe give instruction in this branch of healing. Many books have been written on the subject by eminent medical authorities, and the indications are that during the present century Suggestive Therapeutics, in its various forms, will come even more prominently into popular favor, and that it will be developed far beyond its present limits. Experimental work along these lines is now being conducted in many psychological laboratories in our great universities.

At the same time, as we shall now see, Mental Healing has been attracting much attention along other lines, outside of the medical profession, and often allied with religious and metaphysical movements. To understand the subject, we must study it in all of its phases.

In the early part of the nineteenth century Elijah Perkins, an ignorant blacksmith living in Connecticut conceived a queer idea of curing disease by means of a peculiar pair of tongs manufactured by himself, one prong being of brass and the other of steel. These tongs were called "tractors," and were applied to the body of the patient in the region affected by disease, the body being stroked in a downward direction for a period of about ten minutes. The tractors were used to treat all manner of complaints, ailments and diseases, internal and external, with a wonderful degree of success. Almost miraculous cures of all manner of complaints were reported, and people flocked to Perkins from far and near in order to receive the benefit of his wonderful treatments.

Soon this system of healing came to be called "Perkinsism," as a tribute to the inventor. The popularity of the system spread rapidly in the United States, particularly in New England, every city and many towns patronizing Perkins' practitioners and healers. From this country the craze spread to Great Britain, and even to the Continent. Centers of treatment, and even hospitals, were established by the "Perkinsites," and the fame of the tractors increased daily in ever widening circles. In Europe alone it is reported that over 1,500,000 cures were performed, and the medical fraternity were at their wit's ends to explain the phenomenon. Finally, Dr. Haygarth, of London, conceived the idea that the real virtue of the cures was vested in the minds, belief and imagination of the patients rather than in the tractors, and that the cures were the result of the induced mental states of the patients instead of by the metallic qualities of the apparatus. He determined to investigate the matter under this hypothesis, and accordingly constructed a pair of tractors of wood, painted to resemble the genuine ones. The following account by Bostock describes the result: "He accordingly formed pieces of wood into the shape of tractors and with much assumed pomp and ceremony applied them to a number of sick persons who had been previously prepared to expect something extraordinary. The effects were found to be astonishing. Obstinate pains in the limbs were suddenly cured; joints that had long been immovable were restored to motion, and, in short, except the renewal of lost parts or the change in mechanical structure, nothing seemed beyond their power to accomplish." The exposure of this experiment, and the general acceptance of the explanation of the phenomena, caused "Perkinsism" to die out rapidly, and at the present time it is heard of only in connection with the history of medicine and in the pages of works devoted to the subject of the effect of the mind over the body.

The success of "Perkinsism" is but a typical instance which is duplicated every twenty years or so by the rapid rise, spread and then rapid decline of some new "craze" in healing, all of which, when investigated are seen to be but new examples of the power of the mental states of faith and imagination upon the physical organism. The well-known "blue glass" craze of about thirty-five years ago gives us another interesting example. General Pleasanton, a well-known and prominent citizen of Philadelphia, announced his discovery that the rays of the sun passing through the medium of blue glass possessed a wonderful therapeutic value. The idea fired the public imagination at once, and the General's book met with a large sale. Everyone, seemingly, began to experiment with the blue glass rays. Windows were fitted with blue glass panes, and the patients sat so that the sun's rays might fall upon them after passing through the blue panes. Wonderful cures were reported from all directions, the results of "Perkinsism" being duplicated in almost every detail. Even cripples reported cures, and many chronic and "incurable" cases were healed almost instantaneously. Bedridden people threw aside their blankets and walked again, after a brief treatment. The interest developed into a veritable "craze," and the glass factories were operated overtime in order to meet the overwhelming demand for blue glass, the price of which rapidly advanced to fifty cents and even a dollar for a small pane, because of the scarcity. It was freely predicted that the days of physicians were over, and that the blue glass was the long-sought-for panacea for all human ills. Suddenly, however, and from no apparent cause, the interest in the matter dropped, and now all that is left of the blue glass craze is the occasional sight of an old blue pane in some window, the owner of which evidently felt disinclined to pay the price of replacing it with a clear pane. Only a few days ago, in an old-fashioned quarter of a large city, the writer saw several panes of the old blue glass in the frame of the window of an old house which had seen better days but which was now used as a cheap tenement house.

The history of medicine is filled with records of similar "crazes" following the announcement of some new method of "cure." The striking peculiarity of these cures is that they all occur during the height of the excitement and notoriety of the early days of the announcement, while *they decline in proportion to the decline in public faith and interest*, the explanation being that in every instance the cure is effected by the action of the mental states of expectancy, faith, and the imagination of the patient, irrespective of any virtue in the method or system itself. In short, *all these cures belong to the category of faith-cures*—they are merely duplicates of the world-old cures resulting from faith in sacred relics, shrines, bones of holy people, sacred places, etc., of which nearly every religion has given us many examples. The history of medicine gives us many instances of the efficacy of the therapeutic power of Faith.

Sir Humphrey Davy relates a case in which a man seriously ill manifested immediate improvement after the placing of a clinical thermometer in his mouth, he supposing that it was some new and powerful healing instrument. The grotesque remedies of the ancient physicians, and the *bizarre* decoctions of the quacks of the present, all work cures. The "bread-pills" and other placebos of the "regulars" have cured many a case when other remedies have failed.

It is related that several hundred years ago, a young English law-student while on a lark with several of his boon companions found themselves in a rural inn, without money with which to pay their reckoning. Finally, after much thought, the young man called the inn-keeper and told him that he, the student, was a great physician, and that he would prepare for him a magic amulet which would cure all diseases, in return for the receipted account of himself and friends. The landlord gladly consented, and the young man wrote some gibberish on a bit of parchment, which together with sundry articles of rubbish he inserted in a silk cover. With a wise and dignified air he then departed. Many years rolled by, and the young man rose to the position of a High Justice of the realm. One day before him was brought a woman accused of magic and witchcraft. The evidence showed that she had cured many people by applying to their bodies a little magic amulet, which the church authorities considered to be the work of the devil. The woman, on the stand, admitted the use of the amulet and the many cures resulting therefrom, but defended herself by saying that the instrument of cure had been given to her father, now deceased, many years ago, by a great physician who had stopped at her father's inn. She held that the cures were genuine medical cures resulting from the medicinal virtues of the amulet, and not the result of magic or witchcraft. The Justice asked to be handed the wonderful amulet. Ripping it open with his pen-knife, he found enclosed the identical scrawl inserted by himself many years before. He announced the circumstances from the bench, and discharged the woman—but the healing virtues of the amulet had disappeared, never to return. The cures were the result of the faith and imagination of the patients.

The modern instances of the several great "Divine Healers," such as John Alexander Dowie of Chicago, and Francis Schlatter of Denver, give us additional evidence of the efficacy of Faith as a therapeutic agent. John Alexander Dowie, a Scotch preacher, came to America some twenty years ago, and instituted a new religion in which healing was an important feature. He claimed that all disease was the result of the devil, and that belief in God and the prayers of Dowie and his assistants would work the cure of the devil's evil operations. Great numbers flocked to Dowie's standard, and thousands of wonderful cures were reported. His "Tabernacle" was filled with testimonials and trophies from cured people. Back of Dowie's pulpit were displayed many crutches, plaster-casts, braces, and other spoils wrested from the devil by Dowie and his aids. His experience meetings were thronged with persons willing and anxious to testify that whereas they had been afflicted they were now whole again. Dowie succeeded in building up a great following all over the world, and had he not overreached himself and allowed his colossal vanity to overshadow his original ideas, the probability is that he would have founded a church which would have endured for centuries. As it is, he was discredited and disowned by his followers, and his church is now but little more than a memory.

Francis Schlatter, the German shoemaker of Denver, with his Divine Healing, was a well known figure in the west several years ago. He was undoubtedly a half-insane fanatic, believing himself inspired by God to heal the nations. Persons flocked to him from afar, and he is reported to have healed thousands, many of whom were suffering from serious ailments. He afterward disappeared, and is believed to have died in the desert of the far west. Students of Mental Suggestion and Psychic Therapeutics find in the instances of Dowie and Schlatter merely the same underlying principle of Mental Healing resulting from faith, which is operative in all of the other cases mentioned. The theology, creed, theories of methods have but little to do with the cures, so long as the proper degree of faith is induced in the mind of the patient. Faith in *anything* will work cures, providing it is sufficiently intense and active.

Another branch of Mental Healing is seen in the modern schools of the "New Thought," "Mental Science," "Christian Science," and the "Emmanuel Movement." The authorities generally agree upon tracing the rise of these several schools to the general interest in the subject manifested in the United States and Great Britain about the middle of the last century. Some of the authorities believe that this general interest was induced largely by the teachings of Charles Poyen, a Frenchman who came from France to New England about 1835, bringing with him the French teachings and theories regarding mesmerism and the phenomena allied thereto. Poyen's teachings attracted marked interest and attention, and he soon had a host of followers, students and imitators. Teachers of the "new science" sprang up on all sides. Many theories were evolved and actively supported by the adherents of the several prominent teachers. The rise of interest in phrenology and the dawning interest in spiritualism aided the spread of the new teachings regarding mesmerism, clairvoyance, psychic healing, etc., and the pages of many magazines and books published about that time show that a public taste had been created for the strange and mysterious.

Dr. J. S. Grimes, a physician interested in phrenology, taught that the phenomena were due to the action of a strange atmospheric force which he called "etherium." Rev. J. Bovee Dods evolved a theory based upon the supposed existence of an electrical principle, and called his system "Electro-Biology," by means of which he attracted to himself a large following. Dods wrote several large books on the subject, and traveled on lecture tours in this country and Great Britain, arousing great enthusiasm and making many cures. Rev. Leroy Sunderland expounded the doctrine of "patheism," in which he combined a strange mixture of mysticism and what has since been called "suggestion," to which he afterward added the current teachings of spiritualism after his conversion to that philosophy. It would seem that credit should be given Sunderland for his early announcement of the principle of suggestion, for he said: "When a relation is once established between an operator and his patient, corresponding changes may be induced in the nervous system of the latter by mere volition, and *by suggestions addressed to either of the external senses.*" The decade, 1840-1850 witnessed a remarkable interest in psychic phenomena of all kinds, and during that time there was undoubtedly laid the foundations upon which the later structures have since been erected. Any one reading the short stories of Poe, and other writers of that period, may readily see the state of public interest in these subjects at that time.

The authorities generally agree that in Phineas Parkhurst Quimby we have the direct connecting link between the period just mentioned and the present. Quimby played quite an important role in the evolution of the modern conceptions of mental healing, or psycho-therapy as it is now called. He was a poor clockmaker, of quite limited means, of good character and a strong personality. His education is said to have been limited, but he made up for his lack in this respect by his naturally keen and inquiring mind. In 1838 one of the teachers of mesmerism visited his home in Belfast, Maine, and Quimby attended the seance. He became intensely interested in what he saw, and in the theories propounded, and began to experiment on the people in his town, the result being that he soon acquired a reputation as a powerful mesmerist and a good healer. He followed along the general lines of the "Electro-Biology" theory for a time, and then evolved theories of his own. He cured himself and many others by manual treatment, and was soon kept quite busy in his healing work.

Quimby, thinking deeply regarding the cures he was making, soon came to the conclusion that while his *cures* were genuine, his *theories* were wrong. He gradually evolved the idea that diseases are caused by erroneous thinking, and that his cures resulted from changing these wrong mental states for those based upon true conceptions. He held that all that is required to effect a cure is to bring about "a change of thought." Following upon this new conception, he ceased mesmerizing his patients, and began to treat them by simply sitting by the side of the afflicted person, picturing him as well and whole, and impressing upon the patient's mind that he is well and whole, *in Truth*. From this fundamental idea he gradually evolved a philosophy which has strongly influenced that of later schools. Quimby talked much regarding his great "discovery," as he called it, and built great hopes upon establishing "the science of health and happiness." He began to speak of the "Truth" in his "science," which he held to be identical with that taught by Christ, and by means of which Jesus performed his miraculous cures. Before he had firmly established his "science," however, he died, leaving his work to be carried on by others, notably by Dr. Warren F. Evans, and Julius A. Dresser, to whom should be given the credit for launching what is now known as "the New Thought Movement."

Mrs. Mary Baker G. Eddy, who afterward established "Christian Science" was one of Quimby's patients and students, and Dresser and others have positively stated and claimed that from him she received her ideas of the philosophy which she afterward developed into the great "Christian Science" movement. Mrs. Eddy, and her adherents, as positively deny to Quimby any credit for having inspired Mrs. Eddy's work. We merely state the opposing sides of the controversy here, taking no sides in the matter, the discussion not concerning us in the present consideration.

The success of Evans and Dresser, and of Mrs. Eddy, in their respective schools and organizations, have caused many other teachers to come to the front, until at the present time there are many schools, cults and organizations basing their cures upon the broad principles of Mental Healing. Mrs. Eddy, and her followers, deny having anything in common with the other schools, however, holding that the latter are concerned with "mortal mind" while "Christian Science" alone is based upon Divine Mind, or Truth. In spite of the conflicting claims and theories, the fact remains that thousands of persons have been healed of various diseases by the various schools, cults, and teachings. To the authorities who stand outside of and apart from these opposing organizations, it seems that all the cures are based upon the same general principle, *i. e.*, that of the influence of mental states over physical conditions, and that religious theories or metaphysical philosophies have nothing whatever to do with the production of the cures, except in the direction of giving a strong suggestion to those accepting them. The fact that *all* the schools make cures, in about the same proportion, and of the same general classes of complaints, would seem to show that the theories and dogmas have nothing to do with the process of cure—and that the healing is done *in spite of the theories*, rather than because of them.

The much advertised "Emmanuel Movement" now so popular in the orthodox churches throughout the country, is recognized by all the authorities as being nothing more than suggestion applied in connection with the religious and theological principles of the churches in question, and, in truth, as applying methods more in favor by the old school of mesmerists than by the later "New Thought" practitioners, or by the "Christian Science" healers. From this movement, however, there will probably evolve a more scientific system, manifesting none of the crudities which so disfigure its present stage, at least in the hands of some of its practitioners.

In the following chapter we may see that the same element of Faith, Belief and Expectancy is manifested in all the various forms of Mental Healing, by whatever name, or under whatever theory, the method is applied. In short, that the cures are purely *psychological*, rather than metaphysical or religious, in their nature.

CHAPTER VI

FAITH CURES

Following the scientific study of the phenomena of cures of physical illness by means of the power of mental states, and the recognition of the fact that there is a common principle operative under the various guises and forms, there sprang into scientific usage the term "Faith Cures" which was used to designate all instances and forms of cures coming under the general classification of mental healing. Prof. Goddard defines the term as follows: "A term applied to the practice of curing disease by an appeal to the hope, belief, or expectation of the patient, and without the use of drugs or other material means. Formerly it was confined to methods requiring the exercise of religious faith, such as the 'prayer cure' and 'divine healing,' but has now come to be used in the broader sense, and includes the cures of 'Mental Science,' and hypnotism; also a large part of the cures effected by patent medicines and nostrums, as well as many folk-practices and home remedies. By some it is used to include also Christian Science, but the believers in the latter regard it as entirely distinct."

The term "Suggestion," used in the same sense as "Faith Cure" in relation to the healing of disease, has also come into popular usage, but inasmuch as Suggestion has a much larger meaning outside of its therapeutic phases, it may be said the best authorities to-day use the term "Faith Cure" as representing simply one phase of Suggestion.

Prof. Goddard, in his article on "Faith Cure," in the *New International Encyclopaedia* (Dodd, Mead & Co., New York), says: "Besides these recognized forms (divine healing, mental science, etc.), faith cure is an important element in cures wrought by patent medicines and nostrums, home remedies and folk practices. The advertisement, testimonial of friend, or family tradition arouses the faith of the sick man, and he comes to believe that he needs only to follow directions to be fully cured. The actual value of faith cure as a therapeutic method has been the subject of much discussion. It can no longer be denied that it has value. From divine healing to patent medicine and Father Kneipp's water cure, all cure disease. Each appeals to a particular type of mind, but *the results are practically the same in all—same diseases cured, same successes, same failures.* Many faith-curists claim that all diseases in all persons can be cured by their method; others hold that the principle is of limited application. Of them all, the hypnotists are the only ones who do not make sweeping claims."

After stating "the tendency to exaggeration and the infrequency of impartial judgment" in connection with many instances of claimed cures, the above mentioned authority proceeds as follows: "The actual cures, however, are sufficiently numerous and sufficiently striking to need an explanation. These different forms agree in only one point—viz., *the mental state of the patient is one of hope and expectation.* Can states of mind cause or cure disease? Some familiar occurrences seem to justify an affirmative answer. It is well known that certain glands and secretions are markedly affected by emotions. Fright causes the saliva to cease to flow and the perspiration to start. Sorrow causes the lachrymal glands to secrete tears. Happiness favors digestion, unhappiness retards it. Mosso has demonstrated that the bladder is especially sensitive to emotional states. In general, the pleasant emotions produce an opposite physical effect from the unpleasant ones. There are many glands within the body whose action under emotion we cannot observe; but we may reasonably assume that they also are affected by emotional states. Hence, if unpleasant emotions so act upon the glands as to derange the system and cause disease, the pleasant emotions may reasonably be assumed to tend to restore the normal functions. The various forms of faith cure tend strongly to put the patient in a happy frame of mind—a condition favorable to health. However, there are all degrees of faith and wide differences in the way the system responds to the emotional state. One person is slightly affected by a strong emotion; another is strongly affected by a weak emotion. Hence, there must always be a wide difference in the results of faith-cure methods. The diseases most amenable to faith cure are nervous—including many not recognized as nervous, but having a neural condition as their basis—and functional derangements. Organic diseases are not usually cured, though the symptoms are frequently ameliorated. Chronic diseases due to neuromuscular habit often yield to hypnotic treatment."

Prof. R. P. Halleck says: "Were it not for this power of the imagination, the majority of quack nostrums would disappear. In most cases bread pills, properly labeled, with positive assurances of certain cures accompanying them, would answer the purpose far better than these nostrums, or even much better than a great deal of the medicine administered by regular physicians. Warts have been charmed away by medicines which could have had only a mental effect. Dr. Tuke gives many cases of patients cured of rheumatism by rubbing them with a certain substance declared to possess magic power. The material in some cases was metal; in others wood; in still others, wax. He also recites the case of a very intelligent officer who had vainly taken powerful remedies to cure cramp in the stomach. Then 'he was told that on the next attack he would be put under a medicine which was generally believed to be most effective, but which was rarely used.' When the cramps came on again, 'a powder containing four grains of ground biscuit was administered every seven minutes, while the greatest anxiety was expressed (within the hearing of the party) lest too much be given. Half-drachm doses of bismuth had never procured the same relief in less than three hours. For four successive times did the same kind of attack recur, and four times was it met by the same remedy, and with like success.' A house surgeon in a French hospital experimented with one hundred patients, giving them sugared water. Then, with a great show of fear, he pretended that he had made a mistake and given them an emetic instead of the proper medicine. Dr. Tuke says: 'The result may easily be anticipated by those who can estimate the influence of the imagination. No fewer than eighty—four-fifths—were unmistakably sick.'

"We have a well authenticated case of a butcher, who, while trying to hang up a heavy piece of meat, slipped and was himself caught by the arm upon the hook. When he was taken to a surgeon, the butcher said he was suffering so much that he could not endure the removal of his coat; the sleeve must be cut off. When this was done, it was found that the hook had passed through his clothing close to the skin, but had not even scratched it. A man sentenced to be bled to death was blindfolded. A harmless incision was then made in his arm and tepid water fixed so as to run down it and drop with considerable noise into a basin. The attendants frequently commented on the flow of blood and the weakening pulse. The criminal's false idea of what was taking place was as powerful in its effects as the reality, and he soon died.... There is perhaps not a person living who would not at times be benefited by a bread pill, administered by some one in whom great confidence was reposed."

The same authority also says: "It has been known for a long time that if the attention is directed toward any bodily organ, abnormal sensations may be caused in it, and disease may be developed. The renowned Dr. John Hunter said: 'I am confident that I can fix my attention to any part, until I have a sensation in that part.'" Dr. Tuke says that these "are words which ought to be inscribed in letters of gold over the entrance of a hospital for the Cure of Disease by Psychopathy." Hunter's confident assertion is the more interesting because, drawn from his own experience, it shows that the principle is not confined in its operation to the susceptible and nervous, but operates even on men of the highest mental endowment. We have examples from the literature of the seventeenth century, showing how the expectation of a complaint will produce it. In 1607 an ignorant English physician told a clergyman's wife that she had sciatica, although there was, in reality, nothing the matter with her sciatic nerve. Her attention was thereby directed to it and a severe attack of sciatica was the result. When a person inexperienced in medicine reads carefully the symptoms of some disease, he is apt to begin an attentive search for those symptoms and to end by fancying he has them. Seasick persons have been relieved of their nausea by being made to bail a leaking boat from the fear that it would sink. All their attention was thereby diverted from themselves. Many can recall how children, and grown persons, too, have forgotten all about their alleged intense thirst, as soon as their attention was diverted. Some persons, after eating something which they fancy is a trifle indigestible, center their attention upon the stomach, expecting symptoms of indigestion, and are often not disappointed. A man who had good reason to fear hydrophobia, determined that he would not have it. The pain in the bitten arm became intense, and he saw that he must have something to divert his attention from the wound and his danger. He therefore went hunting, but found no game. To make amends, he summoned a more inflexible will and exerted at every step 'a strong mental effort against the disease.' He kept on hunting until he felt better, and he mastered himself so perfectly that he probably thereby warded off an attack of hydrophobia. Accordingly as we center our attention upon one thing or another, we largely determine our mental happiness and hence our bodily health. One person, in walking through a noble forest, may search only for spiders, and venomous creatures, while another confines his attention to the singing birds in the branches above. One reason why travel is such a cure for diseases of body and mind is because so many new things thereby come in to claim the attention and divert it from its former objects. The following expression from Dr. Tuke should be remembered: '*Thought strongly directed to any part tends to increase its vascularity, and consequently its sensibility.*'"

Dr. C. F. Winbigler says: "The practitioner secures the same effects from a placebo or powdered pop-corn as from some drugs by using suggestion with the former. Every successful physician has used this method at one time or another, and sometimes when he was utterly puzzled as to what he should prescribe, he thus secured a marvellous result, and a cure of the patient was effected.... Every believer in Psychotherapeutics knows that there is a psychical as well as a physical effect from the use of drugs. The psychical value is based on the expectation of their special action, and that which is in the physician's mind may be subtly and powerfully carried over into the patient's mind. The physician's personality, attitude and interest in the patient accomplishes vastly more than the drugs he prescribes or administers. If he is cheerful and hopeful, he gives potency to their action; if he is gloomy, pessimistic and hopeless, he nullifies their effects. The cure of the patient is effected through the subconscious mind, and the attitude and bearings of the physician, attendants, the surroundings and the medicines employed, become powerful suggestions."

Prof. Elmer Gates says: "The system makes an effort to eliminate the metabolic products of tissue-waste, and it is therefore not surprising that during acute grief tears are copiously excreted; that during sudden fear the bowels and the kidneys are caused to act, that during prolonged fear, the body is covered with a cold perspiration; and, that during anger, the mouth tastes bitter, due largely to the increased elimination of sulpho-cyanates. The perspiration during fear is chemically different, and even smells different from that which exudes during a happy mood.... Now if it can be shown in many ways that the elimination of waste products is retarded by sad and painful emotions; nay, worse than that, these depressing emotions directly augment the amount of these poisons. Conversely, the pleasurable and happy emotions, during the time they are active, inhibit the poisonous effects of the depressing moods, and cause the bodily cells to create and store up vital energy and nutritive tissue products."

In an issue of "*The American Practitioner and News*," is reported a discussion before the Lexington (Ky.) Medical and Surgical Society, in which a member, Dr. Guest, related the following experience: "I have a brother-in-law who suffers every summer with hay-fever. He has a relative who believes in Christian Science. She told him that she felt positive that she could direct him to a woman, a Christian Scientist, who would cure him. He at first objected, because he hated to go to a woman physician. He arranged, however, to communicate with her daily by letter. When his hay-fever broke out he suffered with it all that day and night, and the next morning wrote her a note telling her to put him on treatment immediately. When he returned that night he was improved and slept better. He wrote a second note the next morning and was much encouraged. The third day he repeated his letter writing and stated that the symptoms had almost ceased. And he was guying me about being cured by Christian Science when regular physicians could do nothing for him. The night of the third day, when he came home to supper, he found a note from the Christian Scientist, stating that *she has been in the country and would put him under treatment the next day.* Realizing that all his treatment had been only in his imagination, the symptoms reappeared with the same intensity as before."

Dr. A. J. Parks of New York, says: "The absolute and complete control that the sympathetic nervous system exercises over the physical organization is so perfectly clear and well-known to every observer that the recital of the phenomena in the vast and countless series of manifestations is unnecessary. We are all aware of the fact that digestion is promptly arrested upon the receipt of bad news. The appetite at once disappears. It ceases, and the whole system feels the effect of the depressing impulse—the mental and spiritual wave which lowers the vital thermometer. Fear not only suspends the digestive function but arrests the formation of the secretions upon which digestion depends. A sudden fright frequently paralyzes the heart beyond recovery, whereas a pleasant and pleasing message soothes and gently excites the whole granular system, increases the secretions, aids digestion and sends a thrill of joy to the sensorium, which diffuses the glad tidings to every nerve fibril in the complex organization."

Dr. T. A. Borton, in an address before the Indiana State Medical Society, said: "The subject which I desire to present to you to-day has to do with the influence of the mind over the functions of the body. Its silent, unobserved force results in producing pathological conditions, and those, by reflex action, excite morbid sensibilities of the mind and thus derange the nerve centres, resulting in a changed condition or over-excitability of the nerve energies, which becomes a secondary diseased condition in the form of different types of neurasthenia. I have been interested in this subject for many years, and in my practice have had extended opportunities for making observations as to the potency of the mental and suggestive pathology bearing on this subject. I would especially refer to the healing of the body through these mental forces, changing healthy, normal conditions into unhealthy or diseased conditions and *vice versa.* These changes are not miraculous, but proceed from natural causes in the operation of the mind, as a therapeutic agency, operating through the functions of the body, sometimes as a tonic or stimulant, warding off diseases under the most exposed conditions, defending and holding the system in a state of health, while those void of these mental assurances become victims to the ravages of disease through contagion or infection. This protective mental force of the mind has been demonstrated many times in hospitals and other places where contagious diseases were prevailing. The mental force possesses a protective power when rightly exercised beyond what is usually conceded, not only in the way of defense; but also in correcting disease when in existence. I believe these to be much greater than has been generally admitted or understood.... We all know how difficult it is to get good results from medication in which our patients have no confidence, and it is an established fact that we get better results from drugs which are given with the patient's knowledge of their intended effect. *I have often produced desired results from means entirely inert, stating the desired and expected effect of its administration. I have frequently quieted the severest pain by injecting pure water into the arm of the patient.*"

Dr. G. R. Patton, in an address before the Wabasha County (Minn.) Medical Society, said: "As Bacon said, 'Faith, confidence, belief and hope are the working forces that make the cure—that work the miracle.' The mind as a dynamic force exerted over the functions of the body has been, doubtless, operatively manifest from the cradle of our existence. By the phrase, 'the mind as a dynamic force,' I refer to the various forms of suggestion as well as to various affective faculties of the mind, or those states caused by the sympathetic action of the brain, such as faith, confidence, belief, imagination, emotions, hope and the like. Any or all of them may become active over the bodily functions.... As instance of the mental impression acting upon observable functions revealed through the capillary circulation as revealed to the sight, I will mention blushing or pallor of the face, depending upon the theme presented to the thought; the mouth watering on the sight or thought of tempting food; the flow of tears from words or thoughts that excite grief; nausea or vomiting from a sickening spectacle; sexual excitement from obscene thought or lascivious sights. Instances might be multiplied. And is it not a fair inference, indeed, that through the vasomoter nerves, the internal viscera may be subject to like effects through mental impressions, and that thus acute as well as chronic congestive ailments thereof may be favorably influenced or even cured thereby?... It is my conviction that recognition of the power and usefulness of mental dynamics, including all forms of suggestion over physiological and pathological processes in combating diseases, is unquestionably the most impressive advance in modern medicine. Mental influence alone may diminish or increase the activities of the physiological processes to the extent of removing the pathological effects of disease.... A celebrated medical teacher, after an exhaustive dissertation over a case was leaving the bedside without prescribing any treatment when the house physician asked what should be given the patient. 'Oh,' said the professor, 'a hopeful prognosis and anything else you please.' To this he added, 'the doleful doctor will be a failure, while the hopeful one will prove a winner from start to finish.' It is reasonably assured that ultimately the physician will become not so much the man behind the pill as the judicious advisor, the wise counsellor, gently leading the sick 'into green pastures, beside still waters,' through paths that lead onward to recovery, assisting nature at times, if needs be, with a big bread pill."

Dr. Herbert A. Parkyn, the well-known authority on suggestive therapeutics, says: "Certain results will follow certain thoughts, and in every instance that it is possible to get the patient to think the thoughts we desire, we secure the results we desire. It is the work of the suggestionist to place these thoughts in the mind of the patient so that he is bound to think them, and this can be done to some degree, if not perfectly, in every case. It is well to have faith, but faith is not absolutely necessary at the outset. It is time enough for the patient to have faith in the treatment when he can perceive the benefit he is receiving. Understanding the mental and physical changes which follow a certain thought, the suggestionist is able to bring about those mental or physical changes, by using direct suggestion in such a way that his patient is bound to think the thoughts which will produce the results. A man may not have faith in the statement that the thought of lemon juice will stimulate the flow of saliva, but if he will imagine for a moment that he is squeezing the juice of a lemon into his mouth the saliva will immediately flow more freely than usual, regardless of his faith. Similarly, many, if not all of the organs of the body, can be affected by impulses following certain lines of thought, and these impulses will follow the thought and stimulate the organs regardless of faith. It is simply necessary to get a patient to think the proper thoughts, and it is in the thought directing that the work of the suggestionist lies."

CHAPTER VII

THE POWER OF THE IMAGINATION

Dr. F. W. Southworth says: "Fear is itself a contagious disease and is sometimes reflected from one mind to another with great rapidity. It passes from one to another, from the healthy to the ill, from doctor or nurse to patient, from mother to child, and so on. The greatest fears we can usually get away from, but it is the little fears and anxieties, constant apprehension, fears of imagined evils of all sorts which prey upon our vitality and lessen our powers, thus rendering us more susceptible to disease. To avert disease, then, we must eradicate fear; but how shall we accomplish it? Through wise education—educating the people to a higher standard of living; by teaching a sounder hygiene; a wiser philosophy and a more cheerful theology. By erasing a thousand errors and superstitions from fearful minds and pointing them to the light, beauty and loveliness of the truth. This mental and moral sanitation is still ahead of us, but it is more valuable and desirable than all quarantines, inventions, experiments, and microscopical researches after physical or material causes."

Sir George Paget, M. D., says: "In many cases I have seen reasons for believing that cancer has had its origin in prolonged anxiety." Dr. Murchison says: "I have been surprised to find how often patients with primary cancer of the liver have traced the cause of this illness to protracted grief and anxiety. These cases have been far too numerous to be accounted for as merely coincidents." Sir B. W. Richardson, M. D., says: "Eruptions of the skin frequently follow excessive mental strain. In all these, as well as in cancer, epilepsy and mania, the cause is frequently partly or wholly mental. It is remarkable how little the question of the origin of physical disease from mental influences has been studied." Prof. Elmer Gates says: "My experiments show that irascible, malevolent and depressing emotions generate in the system injurious compounds, some of which are extremely poisonous. Also that agreeable, happy emotions generate chemical compounds of nutritious value which stimulate the cells to manufacture energy."

Dr. Patton, in the address before the Wabasha County Medical Society, above mentioned, gives the following interesting case of the effect of faith and expectant attention, or Suggestion: He said: "While surgeon of a Cincinnati hospital one of the messenger boys was often disobedient of orders. The sister superior once asked me how to punish him. I suggested putting him to bed and making him sick with medicine. My advice was acted upon with alacrity. A tea-spoonful of *colored water* was given him every fifteen minutes. With assumed gravity, I ordered the nurse, in the boy's presence, to keep giving the medicine until he became sick and vomited. Within an hour he vomited profusely.... A funny incident illustrative of the faith and confidence sometimes reposed in the medical man and his power in curing disease, happened in my first year of practice. An Irish laborer, much given to profanity, came to my office, with a cold on his chest. I prescribed a soothing mixture and a liniment of camphor, ammonia and soap. A few days later, meeting him on the street, I asked him if the medicine had cured him all right. He replied with enthusiasm, 'Oh! yes, yes, it acted most beautifully and cured me pretty d—— d quick, but it was awful hot stuff, for it burned in my throat like hell-fire itself.' I knew at once, but did not tell him, that he had been swallowing the liniment of camphor, hartshorn and soap, and rubbing the cough mixture on the outside. His faith was even stronger than the liniment, and cured him in spite of the blunder.

"Perhaps the most wonderful confirmation came under my observation while wintering in San Antonio, Texas, in 1880. Some nostrum fakirs with a retinue of fourteen musicians and comedians came to this city in an immense chariot, drawn by eight gaily caparisoned horses. Every evening they came upon the military plaza to sell their panacea. I went over one evening out of curiosity, being attracted by the songs and music. The head fakir was shouting to an immense crowd about the virtues of his specific. He claimed that it contained thirteen ingredients, gathered at a great expense from all quarters of the globe, and would cure all the ills that flesh was heir to. Cures were warranted in every case, or the money refunded on the following evening. After this harangue, he said that the medicine was for sale at $1 per bottle, until 300 bottles had been sold, as it was an invariable rule to sell only that number on any one evening. Immediately a frenzied mob rushed pell-mell to the end of the chariot, each one holding aloft a silver dollar. He had previously announced that no change would be made, and that every one to get the medicine should have a dollar ready in his hand. In half an hour 300 bottles had been sold, the empty trunk closed with a bang, and the statement made that no more could be had until the following evening, although there was yet a great multitude clamoring for more. Curiosity again led me to the plaza the next evening, and I went early. The initial performance was a free tooth-pulling, to last thirty minutes. He said he was the kingpin of the tooth-pullers, and I believe he was. The rapidity of his work was a marvel. He snatched from various jaws about 250 teeth, including the good ones, within the limit, throwing them from his forceps right and left among his audience. Those operated upon were wrought to such a frenzy of excitement and wonder that each one, without an exception, declared that no pain whatever had been experienced. A call was then made for the 300 who had bought medicine on the previous evening to mount the chariot and tell what the medicine had done for them.

"From every quarter men and women, both white and colored, pressed forward to give their experience. Their stories were grotesque and curious enough, but no matter what their ailments, cures had resulted in every case. At the end of half an hour, while the experience meeting was at its acme, the fakir abruptly closed it, saying, in a regretful voice, that the rest would have to wait until the next evening to tell of their cures, as he now wanted those to come forward who had not been cured by the medicine bought on the previous evening. He stood in silence with folded arms for three minutes. No one having come forward, the voice of this arrant charlatan rang out in stentorian tones, 'All, *all* have been cured! We have cured *everyone*!' Then another 300 bottles were sold in a jiffy, I myself being one of the fortunate purchasers. The chief of this outfit stopped in the hotel where I was. After dinner the next day, I made his acquaintance in the smoking room, saying I was a doctor, too; that I had attended two of his soirees, bought his medicine and was greatly interested in it. I surprised him by the statement that his medicine was made by M. & Co., wholesale druggists of Cincinnati, and that it was fluid extract of podophyllin. He stared for some moments, but made no reply. I continued, 'I know M.'s fluid extract, as his process of its manufacture is peculiar, and differs from other manufacturers in this, that he exhausts the root by percolation with alcohol, ether and glycerine, giving the product a sweetish taste and a slight ethereal odor.' The man asked if I was also a chemist. I replied, 'Yes, I once lectured in a medical college in Cincinnati on drugs and their uses, and I can readily tell fluid extracts by their taste, odor and physical characteristics.'

"After some hesitation, he said, 'Yes, this is M.'s podophyllin *and nothing else.*' I inquired if he attributed all his success to the medicine. He answered, 'No, for once in Missouri the mandrake ran out before a new lot arrived. We found something like it in a drug store of the town, and the people got well just the same. *If the people believe you can cure them, and have faith in your medicine, they get well anyway, or they think they do, which is the same thing.*' The fakirs remained one week, sold 2,100 bottles, and presumably cured 2,100 people, as no one came forward to reclaim his dollar for the medicine, which was contained in a two-drachm vial of 120 drops. A dose was one drop after each meal in one spoonful of water.

"When I was in California recently a friend mentioned that an intelligent relative of his was being treated by a celebrated Chinese doctor. The relative claimed that Chinese physicians were better than our own; that they had devoted 5,000 years to medicine and had thus become so learned and skillful that they could tell all diseases without asking a single question, simply by feeling the pulse. Out of curiosity I visited this physician, ostensibly as a patient. Without so declaring myself, he knew intuitively that I came to consult him. Without asking any questions he placed his finger upon my right wrist, communed with himself for a few moments, and then gravely informed me that I had *thirty-seven diseases*; some in the blood, some in the brain, some in the kidneys, some in the liver, and many others in the heart and lungs. He said it would take *sixteen different herbs* to cure me. He volunteered the statement that he could detect 6,000 diseases by the pulse alone, and that he used 400 herbs in the treatment of the various diseases. Upon his request, I examined his portfolio containing 350 testimonials of marvellous cures, wrought upon American residents of California during his seventeen years' practice on the coast. Many of them were from parties of intelligence and eminence, and were so extraordinary that nothing short of their being attested by numerous witnesses of unimpeachable veracity, could satisfy one of their truth. Now, permit me to say that I have no pulse in the right wrist, the pulse being congenitally absent; but through it he made the pretense of locating so many diseases. This doubtless is the form and character of medical practice in China among the native Chinamen, and probably has been for many centuries among a population of 400,000,000. Is not the logic from the above facts irresistible, that in China the native physician cannot tell one disease from another, and that all his work is simply nonsense and guess work? There can be no escape from this conclusion—it follows as lucidly as a demonstrated problem in Euclid—*that* any benefit that may ever accrue from their treatment is wholly due to the dynamic force of the brain upon the functions of the body."

The following, from a Philadelphia journal, gives a striking illustration of the fact that the imagination is a *real* factor in many cases of physical ailment: "The fact that the throes of the imagination under great nervous excitement often produce a corresponding physical frenzy was illustrated recently in the case of a man who had gone to sleep with his artificial teeth in his mouth. Waking suddenly with a choking sensation, he found his teeth had disappeared. He looked in the glass of water where they were usually deposited, did not see them and realized they must be far down his throat. Choking and struggling, he hammered on the door of a friend sleeping in the house, who, seeing his critical condition, vainly tried to draw the teeth out of the sufferer's throat. He could feel the teeth, but had not the strength to extract them. He ran for a blacksmith who lived a few doors away, but the blacksmith's hand was too big to put into the man's mouth. A doctor had been sent for, but he was so long in coming that the victim of the accident seemed likely to die of suffocation before the physician arrived. A little girl of ten years was brought under the impression that her small hand might reach the obstacle and withdraw it, but she got frightened and began to cry. The sufferer became black in the face, his throat swelled out, and his friends expected every moment to be his last, when finally the doctor arrived. He heard the history of the case, saw that the teeth were not in the man's jaws nor in their nightly receptacle, felt the throat and cast his eyes seriously upon the floor. *There, on the floor, he saw the whole set of teeth.* He adjusted them to the jaws of the patient, told him to breathe freely, and every symptom of suffocation disappeared."

The following from an Eastern journal illustrates another phase of the subject: "Saltpetriere, the hospital for nervous diseases, made famous by the investigations of Dr. Charcot, has an interesting case of religious mania. The patient, who is a woman of about forty years of age, entertains the belief that she is crucified, and this delusion has caused a contraction of the muscles of the feet of such a nature that she can walk only on tip-toe. The patient, moreover, is subject occasionally to the still more extraordinary manifestation—that of 'stigmata.' Instances of 'stigmata' are tolerably frequent in the 'Lives of the Saints' of alleged supernatural marks on the body in imitation of the wounds of Christ. These 'stigmata' have been observed beyond all question on the woman at the Saltpetriere. Their appearance on the body coincides with the return of the most solemn religious anniversaries. These 'stigmata' are so visible that it has been possible to photograph them. The doctors of the Saltpetriere in order to assure themselves that these manifestations were not the result of trickery, contrived a sort of shade having a glass front and metal sides, and capable of being hermetically attached to the body by means of India rubber fixings. These shades were placed in position a considerable time before the dates at which the stigmata are wont to appear. When they were affixed there were no marks whatever on the patient's body, but at the expected period the 'stigmata' were visible as usual through the glass."

In a Southern journal there is reported an interesting case, in which a New Orleans physician tells the following story: "A nervous man recently called on me and asked, 'In what part of the abdomen are the premonitory pains of appendicitis felt?' On the *left* side, exactly here,' I replied, indicating a spot a little above the point of the hip-bone. He went out, and next afternoon I was summoned in hot haste to the St. Charles hotel. I found the planter writhing on his bed, his forehead beaded with sweat, and his whole appearance indicating intense suffering. 'I have an attack of appendicitis,' he groaned, 'and I'm a dead man! I'll never survive an operation!' 'Where do you feel the pain?' I asked. 'Oh, right here,' he replied, putting his finger on the spot I had located at the office. 'I feel as if somebody had a knife in me turning it around.' 'Well, then, it isn't appendicitis, at any rate,' I said cheerfully, 'because *it is the wrong side.*' 'The wrong side!' he exclaimed, glaring at me indignantly. 'Why, you told me yourself it was on the *left* side!' 'Then I must have been abstracted,' I replied calmly; 'I should have said the *right* side.' I prescribed something that wouldn't hurt him, and learned afterward that he ate his dinner in the dining-room the same evening. Oh! yes; he was no doubt in real pain when I called, *but you can make your finger ache merely by concentrating your attention on it for a few moments.*"

Frank F. Moore, in "A Journalist's Note Book" tells the following amusing and significant story of the influence of imagination upon health. "A young civil servant in India, feeling fagged from the excessive heat and from long hours of work consulted the best doctor within reach. The doctor looked him over, sounded his heart and lungs, and then said gravely: 'I will write you tomorrow.' The next day the young man received a letter telling him that his left lung was gone and his heart seriously affected, and advising him to lose no time in adjusting his business affairs. 'Of course, you may live for weeks,' the latter said, 'but you had best not leave important matters undecided.' Naturally the young official was dismayed by so dark a prognosis—nothing less than a death warrant. Within twenty-four hours he was having difficulty with his respiration, and was seized with an acute pain in the region of the heart. He took to his bed with the feeling that he should never rise from it. During the night he became so much worse that his servant sent for the doctor. 'What on earth have you been doing to yourself?' demanded the doctor. 'There were no indications of this sort when I saw you yesterday?' 'It is my heart, I suppose,' weakly answered the patient. 'Your heart!' repeated the doctor. 'Your heart was all right yesterday.' 'My lungs, then.' 'What is the matter with you, man? You don't seem to have been drinking?' 'Your letter,' gasped the patient.

'You said I had only a few weeks to live.' 'Are you crazy?' said the doctor. 'I wrote you to take a few weeks vacation in the hills, and you would be all right.' For reply the patient drew the letter from under the bedclothes and gave it to the doctor. 'Heavens!' cried that gentleman as he glanced at it. 'This was meant for another man! My assistant has mixed up the letters.' The young man at once sat up in bed and made a rapid recovery. And what of the patient for whom the direful prognosis was intended? Delighted with the report that a sojourn in the hills would set him right, he started at once, and five years later was alive and in fair health."

The following is clipped from a medical journal: "Some physician makes use of this suggestive phrase—'the dynamic power of an idea,' and, as an illustration of what is meant by this expression, the following incident is related. Not long ago a man in taking medicine was suddenly possessed by the notion that he had by mistake taken arsenic. His wife insisted to the contrary, but he proceeded to manifest all the peculiar symptoms of arsenical poisoning, and finally died. So certain was his wife that he had not taken arsenic that an autopsy was held, when not an atom of the poison could be found. Of what did this man die? Arsenic? No, of the dynamic power of an idea or arsenic. Happily for humanity this dynamic power of ideas works constructively no less certainly than it does destructively, and an idea of health fixed in the consciousness and persistently adhered to would tend to bring the best results. Over a hundred years ago, old John Hunter said, '*As the state of mind is capable of producing disease, another state of it may effect a cure.*'"

Dr. William C. Prime relates the following case in his book "Among the Northern Hills." "The judge was summoned in a hurry to see an old lady who had managed her farm for forty years since her husband's death. She had two sons, and a stepson, John, who was not an admirable person. After a long drive on a stormy night the judge found the old lady apparently just alive, and was told by the doctor in attendance to hurry, as his patient was very weak. The judge brought paper and ink with him. He found a stand and a candle, placed them at the head of the bed, and after saying a few words to the woman, told her he was ready to prepare the will if she would go on and tell him what she wanted him to do. He wrote the introductory phrase rapidly, and leaning over toward her said, 'Now, go on, Mrs. Norton.'

"Her voice was quite faint, and she seemed to speak with an effort. She said: 'First of all, I want to give the farm to my sons, Harry and James. Just put that down.' 'But,' said the judge, 'you can't do that, Mrs. Norton. The farm isn't yours to give away.' 'The farm isn't mine?' she said in a voice decidedly stronger than before. 'No, the farm isn't yours. You have only a life interest in it.' 'This farm that I've run for goin' on forty-three year next spring isn't mine to do with what I please with it? Why not, Judge I'd like to know what you mean!' 'Why, Mr. Norton, your husband, gave you a life estate in all his property, and on your death the farm goes to his son, John, and *your* children get the village houses. I have explained that to you very often before.' 'And when I die, John Norton is to have this house and farm whether I will or not?' 'Just so. It will be his.' '*Then I ain't goin' to die!*' said the old woman, in a clear and decidedly ringing and healthy voice. And so saying, she threw her feet over the front of the bed, sat up, gathered a blanket and coverlet about her, straightened her gaunt form, walked across the room and sat down in a great chair before the fire.

"The doctor and the judge went home. That was fifteen years ago. *The old lady is alive to-day.* And she accomplished her intent, She beat John after all. He died four years ago."

CHAPTER VIII

BELIEF AND SUGGESTION

The writer has been informed by a prominent physician of Chicago, that for many years he has been in the habit of administering hypodermic injections of distilled water, accompanying the same by the statement that he is injecting morphine. He states that in every case, he has succeeded in inducing a quiet, peaceful sleep, and a cessation of pain after the injection, which can be attributed only to the *belief* of the patient. The same physician also relates the case of a woman who believed that she had taken strychnine by mistake. When the doctor was called he found the woman manifesting every symptom of strychnine poisoning, even down to the most minute details, and he is of the opinion that death would have ensued in a short time had he not proceeded to administer the regular antidotes and restorative treatment. After the woman was brought out of the condition, it was discovered that the supposed strychnine was nothing but a harmless powder. In relating the case, the physician always adds that the woman had witnessed the death struggles of a dog which had been poisoned by strychnine several months previous, which might have had some effect in enabling her to unconsciously counterfeit the symptoms.

Dr. Max Eastman, in a recent magazine article says: "The mission of this paper is to offer guidance in a matter about which a great quantity of the general public is very much at sea. In this question of 'mind over matter,' the reformers have done their work. They have stirred things up. They have bestowed upon the world about a hundred and fifty little religions and a confused idea that there must be some truth in the matter somewhere. The ignorant have done their work. They have persecuted the believers, jeered at them, or damned them with a vacuous smile. The world will never lack ballast. It is only the scientists that have failed of their duty. They have stalked through a routine of elevated lectures, written a few incomprehensible books, and kept the science of psychology, so far as the hungry world goes, sealed up in their own proud bosoms. In all this uproar of faith-cures, and miracles, and shouting prophets, we have heard few illuminating words from the universities. The consequence is that we are without a helm, and the reform blows now one way and now another....

"The law of suggestion, which is one of the great discoveries of modern science, was first formulated by Dr. Liebault at Paris, in a book published in 1866. Since his day the number of physicians who practice 'suggestive therapeutics' has steadily increased, until to-day no thorough clinical hospital is without a professional suggestionist. The practice *does not involve any metaphysical theories*, the passage of any hidden force from one brain to another, any 'planes of existence,' or any religious upset, or any poetic physiology, or the swallowing of any occult doctrines whatever. It is one of the simplest and coolest of scientific theories. It is a question of the relation between the brain and the bodily organs. It seems never to have been clearly stated that healing disease by suggestion depends not in the least degree upon any theory of the relation of mind and matter.... The attempt to fix an idea in the mind without reason is suggestion. It is accomplished usually in medical practice by asking the patient to lie down and relax his body and his mind and then vigorously stating to him the desired idea. It may be accomplished in a number of ways. The patient may be told that the operator is a wizard and is about to transfer an idea from his own mind to that of the patient. If the patient believes him he will very likely accept the idea. It may be accomplished by gestures or incantations which the patient regards with superstitious awe, provided it is explained beforehand what these gestures are meant to produce. It may be accomplished by telling the patient he has no body, and sitting with him for awhile in spiritual silence, *provided he knows what to expect*.

"All these methods, *if one believes in them*, are good, and they prove by their success the law of suggestion. But the method that is based on a sure truth is the method of the scientist. He reasons with his patient, he stirs in him what moral or religious enthusiasm he can, and to these means he adds tactfully the subtle suggestive powers of his own presence and eloquence. This force, together with the power which is revealed in a man of correcting his own mental habits, is the greatest practical discovery of modern psychology.... Suggestive therapeutics is the use of suggestion to fix in the mind ideas of healthy mental habits....

"Our question is: can the physical conditions of the brain affect the physical condition of the stomach? We know that the brain-building condition which accompanies the idea of raising our hand can affect the condition of the muscles of our arm—and we call that a voluntary function. Now the question is whether the brain condition which accompanies the idea of enlivening our stomach can have an effect upon that involuntary function. Experiments with suggestion have proved that in some cases it can, if it continues long enough. Persons of a very suggestible nature, can, for instance, by concentrating their mind upon a certain part of the body, increase the flow of blood to that part, although the regulation of blood flow is supposed to be entirely involuntary. The action of the heart, also the movements of the digestive organs particularly, and of the organs of elimination, are almost directly affected in suggestible persons by that change in their brains which accompanies certain ideas.... Science has established then, that suggestion can effect to some extent, the so-called involuntary functions of the body; but the extent or limitation of these effects is by no means determined. It could not be determined scientifically without years of diligent experiment and tabulation. Any dogmatic statement upon one side or the other of that question, is therefore premature and against the spirit of science."

Dr. Leith, in his Edinburgh lectures in 1896, said: "I am inclined to doubt whether the benefits of Nauheim (a treatment for the heart) is not after all to be explained largely, if not entirely, by the influence of the mental factor." Tuke says that: "John Hunter says he was subject to spasm of his 'vital parts' when anxious about an event; as, for instance, whether his bees would swarm or not, whether the large cat he was anxious to kill would get away before he could get the gun. After death it was found that he had some heart disease.... Lord Eglinton told John Hunter how, when two soldiers were condemned to be shot, it was arranged the one who threw the number with the dice should be reprieved; the one who proved successful generally fainted, while the one to be shot remained calm." Dr. Schofield says: "During the rush of Consumptives to Berlin for inoculation by Dr. Koch's tuberculin, a special set of symptoms were observed to follow the injection and were taken as being diagnostic of the existence of tuberculosis; among others, a rise of temperature after so many hours. These phenomena were eagerly looked for by the patients, and occurred accurately in several who were injected with pure water. The formation of blisters full of serum from the application of plain stamp and other paper to various parts of the bodies of patients in the hypnotic state, is well attested and undoubtedly true."

Dr. Krafft-Ebing has produced a rise from 37 degrees centigrade to 38.5 degrees centigrade in patients by fixing their minds by suggestion. In the same way Binet lowered the temperature 10 degrees centigrade. The latter authority says: "How can it be, when one merely says to the patient: 'Your hand will become cold,' and the vaso-motor system answers by constricting the artery? *C'est ce que depasse notre imagination.*" Schofield commenting on the above, says: "Indeed there is no way of accounting for such a phenomena but by freely admitting the presence of unconscious psychic forces in the body, capable of so influencing the structures of the body as to produce physical changes." Tuke says: "A lady saw a child in immediate danger of having its ankle crushed by an iron gate. She was greatly agitated, but could not move, owing to intense pain coming on in her corresponding ankle. She walked home with difficulty, took off her stocking and found a circle around the ankle of a light red color, with a large red spot on the outer side. By the morning her whole foot was inflamed, and she had to remain in bed for some days. A young woman witnessing the lancing of an abscess in the axilla immediately felt pain in that region, followed by inflammation. Dr. Marmise of Bordeaux tells us of a lady's maid, who when the surgeon put his lancet into her mistress's arm to bleed her, felt the prick in her own arm, and shortly after there appeared a bruise at the spot."

It is related that St. Francis d'Assisi dwelt so long in concentrated meditation upon the thought and picture of the Crucifixion that he suffered intense pain in his hands and feet, at the points corresponding to the place of the nails in the hands and feet of Christ, which was afterward followed by marked inflammation at those points, terminating in actual ulceration. The phenomena of the *stigmata* in the cases of religious enthusiasts and fanatics has been mentioned elsewhere in this book. Prof. Barrett says of the phenomenon: "It is not so well known, but it is nevertheless the fact, that utterly startling physiological changes can be produced in a hypnotized subject merely by conscious or unconscious mental suggestion. Thus a red scar or a painful burn, or even a figure of a definite shape, such as a cross or an initial, can be caused to appear on the body of the entranced subject solely through suggesting the idea. By creating some local disturbance of the blood-vessel in the skin, the unconscious self has done what would be impossible for the conscious to perform. And so in the well-attested cases of *stigmata*, where a close resemblance to the wounds of the body of the crucified Saviour appears on the body of the ecstatic. This is a case of unconscious self-suggestion, arising from the intent and adoring gaze of the ecstatic upon the bleeding figure on the crucifix."

Dr. Schofield says: "The breath is altered by the emotions. The short quiet breath of joy contrasts with the long sigh of relief after breathless suspense. Joy gives eupnœa or easy breathing, grief or rather fear tends to dyspnœa or difficult breathing. Sobbing goes with grief, laughter with joy, and one often merges into the other. Yawning is produced by pure idea or by seeing it, as well as by fatigue. Dr. Morton Prince says a lady he knew always had violent catarrh in the nose (hay fever) if a rose was in the room. He gave her an *artificial* one and the usual symptoms followed. How many cases of hay-fever have a somewhat similar origin in the unconscious mind?... The hair may be turned grey and white by emotion in a few hours or sooner. With regard to the stomach and digestion, apart from actual disease, we may notice one or two instances of unconscious mind action. A man who was very sea-sick lost a valuable set of artificial teeth overboard, and was instantly cured. If the thoughts are strongly directed to the intestinal canal, as by bread-pills, it will produce strong peristaltic action. Vomiting occurs from mental causes, apart from organic brain disease. Bad news will produce nausea; emotion also, or seeing another person vomit, or certain smells or ideas, or thoughts about a sea-voyage, etc., or the thought that an emetic has been taken.... The thought of an acid fruit will fill the mouth with water. A successful way of stopping discordant street music is to suck a lemon within a full view of a German band. Fear will so dry the throat that dry rice cannot be swallowed. This is a test in India for the detection of a murderer. The suspected man is brought forward and given a handful of dry rice to swallow. If he can do this he is innocent; if he cannot he is guilty, fear having dried up his mouth.... A young lady who could not be cured of vomiting was engaged to be married. On being told that the wedding day must be postponed till cured, the vomiting ceased.... A mother nursing her child always found the milk secreted when she heard the child crying for any length of time. Fear stops the secretion of milk, and worry will entirely change its character, so as to become absolutely injurious to the child."

Maudsley says: "Perhaps we do not as physicians consider sufficiently the influence of mental states in the production of disease, their importance as symptoms; or realize all the advantages which we take of them in our efforts to cure disease. Quackery seems to have got hold of a truth which legitimate medicine fails to appreciate or use adequately." Dr. Buckley says: "A doctor was called to see a lady with severe rheumatism, and tried to extemporize a vapor bath in bed, with an old tin pipe and a tea-kettle; and only succeeded in scalding the patient with the boiling water proceeding from the overful kettle through the pipe. The patient screamed: 'Doctor, you have scalded me,' and leaped out of bed. But the rheumatism was cured, and did not return." Tuke relates an amusing instance of the effect of suggestion and faith upon warts. He had been considering the subject of the various "pow-wows" or "wart-cures" of the old women, and determined to try some experiments in order to see whether these cures were not due simply to mental influences and expectant attention. On an official tour he visited an asylum, where he was regarded as a great personage by reason of his office. He noticed that several of the inmates were afflicted with warts, and muttering a few words over the excresences, he told the owners that by such and such a day the warts would have completely disappeared. He forgot the circumstances, owing to the press of his official duties, and was agreeably surprised when, on his next round of visits, he was told that his patients had been cured at the time he had predicted. Nearly everyone has had some personal acquaintance with some of these "pow-wow" wart cures, in one form or another. Tying a knot in a piece of cord, then rubbing the wart with it, and burying the string, has cured thousands of cases of warts—the suggestion being the real cause behind the mask.

Ferassi cured fifty cases of ague by a charm, which consisted merely of a piece of paper with the word "Febrifuge" written on it. The patient was directed to clip off one letter of the word each day until cured. Some patients recovered as soon as the first "F" was clipped from the paper. The writer hereof knows personally of a number of people having been cured of fever and ague by means of a written "charm" which an old man in Philadelphia sold them at a dollar a copy. The old man informed him that he, "and his father before him" had cured thousands of people in this way, making a comfortable living from the practice. Dr. Gerbe, of Paris, cured 401 out of 629 cases of toothache by masked suggestion administered in the form of causing the patients to crush a small insect between their fingers, after having strongly impressed upon them the fact that this was an infallible cure.

Dr. Schofield reports the following interesting cases of cures by auto-suggestion and faith: "A surgeon took into a hospital ward some time ago, a little boy who had kept his bed for five years, having hurt his spine in a fall. He had been all the time totally paralyzed in the legs, and could not feel when they were touched or pinched; nor could he move them in the least degree. After careful examination, the doctor explained minutely to the boy the awful nature of the electric battery, and told him to prepare for its application the next day. At the same time he showed him a sixpence, and sympathizing with his state, told him that the sixpence should be his if, notwithstanding, he should have improved enough the next day to walk leaning on and pushing a chair, which would also save the need of the battery. In two weeks the boy was running races in the park, and his cure was reported in the '*Lancet*.' ... A young lady who had taken ether three and a half years before, on the inhaler being held three inches away from the face, and retaining a faint odor of ether, went right off, and becoming unconscious without any ether being used or the inhaler touching her face. A woman was brought on a couch into a London hospital by two ladies, who said she had been suffering from incurable paralysis of the spine for two years, and having exhausted all their means in nursing her, they now sought to get her admitted, pending her removal to a home for incurables. In two hours I had cured her by agencies which owed all their virtue to their influence on the mind, and I walked with the woman half a mile up and down the waiting-room, and she then returned home in an omnibus, being completely cured. An amusing case is that of a paralyzed girl, who on learning that she had secured the affections of the curate, who used to visit her, got out of bed and walked—cured; and soon afterwards made an excellent pastor's wife. A remarkable instance of this sort of cure is that of a child afflicted with paralysis, who was brought up from the country to Paris to the Hotel Dieu. The child, who had heard a great deal of the wonderful metropolis, its magnificent hospitals, its omnipotent doctors, and their wonderful cures, was awe-struck, and so vividly impressed with the idea that such surroundings must have a curative influence, that the day after her arrival she sat up in bed much better. The good doctor just passed around, but had not time to treat her till the third day; by which time when he came round she was out of bed, walking about the room, quite restored by the glimpses she had got of his majestic presence."

Having now shown by numerous disinterested authorities, the majority of whom belong to the medical profession, that the mental states of belief, faith and expectancy, and their negative aspects of fear, apprehension, and false-belief, may, and do, influence physical conditions, functioning and activities, irrespective of the particular theory, creed, or explanation accepted by the patient himself, or herself, we see the necessity of seeking for the common principle of cure manifesting in the various forms of phenomena. And before this common principle may be grasped, we must needs acquaint ourselves with the physical organism involved in the process of cure. Accordingly the several succeeding chapters will be devoted to that phase of the general subject.

CHAPTER IX

PSYCHO-THERAPEUTIC METHODS

The reader will have seen from the preceding chapters that we have proceeded upon the theory that Suggestion is the universal operative principle manifesting in all forms of mental healing, under whatever guise the latter may be presented and by whatever method it may be applied. But it must be remembered that by "Suggestion" we do not mean the theories of any particular group of psycho-therapists, but rather the broad general principle indicated by that term which operates in the direction of influencing the Subconscious Mind and its activities. Let us consider the principle of Suggestion that we may understand what it is, and what it is not.

The term "Suggestion" has as its root the Latin word *suggero*, which is translated as follows: *sug* (or *sub*), "under;" and *gero*, "to carry;" that is, "to carry or place under." In its general usage it signifies "The introduction indirectly into the mind or thoughts; or that which is so introduced." Ordinarily a "suggestion" is an idea indirectly insinuated into the mind, and generally without the process of argument or reasoning. In the New Psychology, the term "suggestion" is used in the sense of an idea which is "carried under" the objective or conscious mind, and introduced to the subjective or Subconscious Mind. In Suggestive Therapeutics, a "suggestion" is an idea introduced into that part of the Subconscious Mind which governs and controls the physical functions and activities, and which is embodied in the cells and cell-groups of the body as we have stated in the preceding chapters.

By many mental healers the term "Suggestion" is applied only to the particular method of applying Suggestion employed by physicians and others who practice under the general theories of Suggestive Therapeutics, and the first mentioned class deny that they use Suggestion because, as they say, they do not use the methods of the practitioners of Suggestive Therapeutics, and make their cures by "metaphysical" or "spiritual" means, or according to some creed or metaphysical theory which, accepted, works the cure. We think that the unprejudiced reader who has followed us this far will have seen that these metaphysical theories, creeds, and special dogmas are simply the outward mask of Suggestion. These healers simply supply a form of Suggestion which is acceptable to the patient because of his temperament, training, etc., and the healing process operates along the lines of the "faith cure."

The fact that healers of entirely opposite theories and doctrines manage to make cures in about the same proportion and in about the same time, would seem to prove that the theories or dogmas have but little to do with the real work of healing. Whatever form of Suggestion is most acceptable to the patient, will best perform the healing work in that particular case. This will also serve to explain why some patients failing to obtain relief from one school of mental healing often are cured by healers of another school, and *vice versa.* Some need Suggestion couched in the mystical terms of some of the cults; others need it garbed in religious drapings, while others prefer some vague metaphysical theory which seems to explain the phenomena. Others still are repelled by any of the above forms, but respond readily to the Suggestion of a physician administering "straight" suggestive treatment, without any religious, metaphysical, or mystical disguise. In all of these cases the real healing work is done by the Subconscious Mind of the patient himself, the various forms of Suggestion serving merely to awaken and rouse into activity the latent forces of nature.

We invite your consideration of the following forms of "treatment" for various disorders, as given by some of the "Divine Scientists" and other metaphysical and semi-religious organizations and cults. As you read them, try to discover the Suggestive germ so nicely surrounded by the sugar-coating—the Suggestive pill so cleverly concealed by the "metaphysical" raisin.

From a journal published in Chicago several years ago, called "Universal Truth," the following "treatments" were clipped:

A correspondent who asked for a "treatment" adapted to the cure of *nervousness,* is instructed to use the following formula, which must be "repeated over and over":

"I am warmed and fed and clothed and healed by Divine Love."

Another correspondent is given the following formula for the cure of sore feet, the affirmation to be made frequently:

"I so thoroughly understand the divine working of the Truth, and I so thoroughly realize the presence of the Father in me and about me that I am now conscious that omnipotent Love rules in every atom of my being, soul and body. My feet can never be weary

nor sore. God created my feet perfect. I walk the pathway of life in perfect ease and comfort. All the obstacles in my path have vanished, and my feet are bathed in a sea of pure love. Through a knowledge and realization of the presence of Omnipotence, I praise and thank God for the perfect spirit of peace that now dwells within me."

The following additional "treatment" is suggested to this sufferer from *sore feet*:

"*Mentally place yourself in an attitude to realize the power of the words you utter, for the fullness of peace and harmony in your feet comes with realization. The more frequently this spiritual medicine is used, the sooner comes manifestation of perfect health.*"

The same journal contained the following item:

"The following invigorating affirmations are used at the Exodus Club, Chicago, Sunday mornings, the congregation repeating them after the leader: '*With reverent recognition of my birthright, I claim my sonship with the Almighty. I am free from disease and disorder. I am in harmony with my source. The Infinite Health is made manifest in me. The Infinite Substance is my constant supply. The Infinite Life fills and strengthens me. The Infinite Intelligence illumines and directs me. The Infinite Love surrounds and protects me. The Infinite Power upholds and supports me. I am out of bondage. I have the freedom of the sons of God. With all that is in me I rejoice and give thanks. God and man are the all in all, now and forever more.*'"

The same journal recommends the following affirmations for general health treatment:

"Monday—*Perfect health is my external birthright.*

"Tuesday—*I have health of intellect, therefore I have wise judgment and clear understanding.*

"Wednesday—*I am morally healthful, therefore in all my dealings I love to realize that I am quickened by the spirit of integrity.*

"Thursday—*Healthfulness of soul gives me a pure heart and righteousness of motive in everything I do.*

"Friday—*Meditation upon the health of my real being outpictures in physical health and strength, in even temper, joyous spirits and in kind words.*

"Saturday—*My health is inexhaustible, because I keep my eye steadily fixed upon its eternal Principle, and my mouth filled with words of its Omnipotence.*

"Sunday—*The Father and I are one; one in purpose, alike in Substance, and one in manifestation.*"

In the same journal a correspondent gives the following treatment for *rupture*:

"*You were conceived in Divine Love. You are the expression of that pure, perfect Love. Divine Love is a binding, cementing power. It is the power that holds all atoms in their places. Every atom of your body is drawn and held together in its place by this power. If any of them get separated as by rupture or any other appearance, they may be drawn together and cemented by the omnipotent power of Love; but the word must be spoken. Therefore use the following: 'The omnipotent spirit of Love in me heals this rupture and gives me peace.' Then, mentally realize the truth of your words, for the Spirit alone can heal.*"

The following treatment for *appendicitis* is given in the same journal:

"*The false theories of physicians and surgeons, and the general impressions regarding that error named Appendicitis are powerless to produce or perpetuate such manifestation. The great law of harmony reigns and only waits the universal acknowledgment of its supremacy to obliterate all such falsity, thereby obliterating the manifestation. We claim, therefore, freedom from such error for every soul. We make this claim in the name of Jesus Christ."*

From the same source is taken this treatment for *periodical nausea in a child*:

"Dear child, every organ of your body is designed to represent the ideal and perfect organ in your real spiritual being; and every function of your body must respond to the word of truth which is now sent forth to establish harmony in your consciousness. The infinite Love that is omnipresent and all-powerful permeates and penetrates every organ and function of your body, and corrects every tendency to discord or disease. By that infinite Love you are now made free. You are fearless and free. You are joyous and free. You are free from the fear of others. You manifest health, strength and peace. Harmony reigns in mind and body. The word of truth has made you free."

Also the following treatment for *constipation*:

"I do realize that the power of divine Love so permeates every atom of my being that my bowels move freely and without effort. This inflowing of divine Love removes all obstructions and I am healed. I realize joy and eternal life so fully that the spirit of Peace is ever present with me. I acknowledge the fullness of joy, peace and power, and have come into a realization of my oneness with infinite Spirit; therefore I rest in thee, O my father."

Another journal of "Divine Science" gave the following "Health Thought" to be held during the month:

"All the natural channels of my body are open and free. The substance of my body is good."

Also the following treatment for *general health*:

"What is true of God is true of man. God is the One All, and is always in a state of wholeness. I, the man of God, am always whole, like unto the One All. No false belief environs or limits me. No shadow darkens my mental vision. My body is a heavenly body, and my eyes do behold the glory of God in all visible things.

I am well, and provided for, thank God, and nothing can make me think otherwise."

While to the orthodox practitioner of medicine the above affirmation and "treatments" may seem to be nothing but a ridiculous conglomeration of mystical, religious and metaphysical terms, without sequence, logical relation, or common-sense, *it is true that statements and treatments similar to the above have successfully healed many cases of physical ailments.* There are thousands of people who will testify that they were healed in a similar manner, and the majority of them believed that there was some particular and peculiar virtue in the formula used, or in the theories and beliefs upon which the formula was based. But the unprejudiced student of Suggestion will readily see that the real healing force was with the mind and being of the patients themselves, and that the *faith, belief and expectant attention* was aroused by the formula and the theories. The principle is that of all Faith Cures—the principle of Suggestion.

Other schools of metaphysical or religious healers treat the patient by impressing upon his mind the fact that God being perfect, good and loving could not be guilty of creating evil, pain or disease, and that such things are non-existent in the "Divine Mind," and are merely illusion, errors, or false claims of the "mortal mind," or "carnal mind" of the patient; therefore, if the patient will deny their reality, and will admit as existent only such things as are held in the Divine Mind, *i. e.*, the *good* things, then the evil things, being merely illusions and untruths, must of necessity fade away and disappear and perfect health will result. Others treat their patients by impressing upon their minds the idea that sickness and disease is either the world or "the devil," or of the "principle of evil," the latter being described as "the negation of truth," and similar terms; and that therefore fixing the mind and faith upon the "principle of Good," or God, must result in driving away the evil conditions. Others hold that disembodied spirits are aiding in the cure. There are thousands of variations rung on the chimes of metaphysical or religious suggestions in the cults. *And they all make some cures*, remember—*in spite of their theories* rather than because of them.

The Mental Scientists come nearest to the ideas of the New Psychology, when they teach that "As a man thinketh, so is he," and that the mind of man creates physical conditions, good and evil, and that the constant holding of the ideal of perfect health and the assertion thereof, will restore normal healthy conditions to the person suffering from physical ailments. Mental Science is very near to being "straight suggestion" so far as the actual method of treatment is concerned, although it resembles some of the other cults when it begins to speculate or dogmatize regarding the nature of the universe, etc.

Differing from these metaphysical, mystical, or religious schools of healing in theory, although employing the same principle, we find the school of Suggestive Therapeutics, proper, favored by many of the regular physicians and by a number of other healers who base their treatment upon the idea of "straight suggestion" coupled with hygienic truth and rational physiological facts. Perhaps a better idea of the theories and ideas of this school may be obtained by referring to the actual treatments given by some of their leading practitioners.

Herbert A. Parkyn, M. D., an eminent practitioner of Suggestive Therapeutics, gives the following instruction to his pupils: "Students often ask for information as to what they should say to a patient when thorough relaxation is realized. As no two cases are exactly alike, it follows that the suggestions given must necessarily fit the case, and be given with a view to bring about the mental and physical condition desired. For instance, in treating a patient who is afflicted with insomnia, suggestions of sleep should be persistently given; and in cases of malnutrition suggestions of hunger should be made to stimulate the appetite for food. The operator should bear in mind that *the reiteration of the suggestion that will change the condition existing, to that desired, is always the right one*, and his own intelligence will be the best guarantee as to what the suggestion should be.... Always arouse the expectant attention of a patient.... So logical a line of argument can be made that each patient will have a reason for expecting certain conditions to be brought about. *With the patient's attention on the desired results, they generally come to pass.* It is better not to give negative suggestions, such as, 'You will not, or cannot do this, that or the other thing,' etc. Pointing out what is not desirable does not suffice. In place of such suggestions, tell what you really wish your patients to do. For example, if a man should mount his bicycle incorrectly, he would profit nothing if we should merely tell him that the way he mounted was not the proper one. How much easier it would be for all concerned if the proper manner of mounting should be shown at once. Just so it is with therapeutic suggestions, *keep suggesting the conditions of mind or body you wish to bring about.*"

The following treatment given as an example by F. W. Southworth, M. D., in his little book on "True Metaphysical Science, and its Practical Application through the Law of Suggestion," furnishes an excellent illustration of the form of suggestive treatment favored by this particular school. The patient is addressed as follows:

"As thoughts are not only things, but forces and act upon our mental and physical life for good or ill, we must be careful to always keep ourselves in that condition of thought which builds up and strengthens, to constantly think thoughts of *health*, of *happiness*, of *good*, to be *cheerful*, hopeful, confident and fearless. (Repeat five or six times.) In order to sustain this condition of positive thinking it requires the development of the will power. The will is the motive power and the controlling force in all aspects of our life, but we develop it especially for the concentration and control of thought. This is the higher self—the infinite will. Exercise it with vigor and earnest persistency, and learn to *rely* upon it. Assert its power as you assert the power of the muscles in exercise and it will manifest itself and the thought will be positive, the secretions of the body will be normal, and the circulation of the blood in the head will be kept at that proper equilibrium which insures the constant nutrition of the cells of the brain and their constant vigor and strength of control of all the organs and tissues of the body, and this vast and intricate machinery of the body will work harmoniously for the production of nutrition through elaboration of the food elements.

"As our body is constantly changing and wasting, we must rebuild and restore it constantly, and we do so from the air we breathe, the water we drink, and the food we eat. The most important of these is the air you breathe, as it is not only a food in itself to the tissues, but it vitalizes the food you eat and the water you drink. Give it that quality of your thought and breathe it as you have been directed at least six times per day for a period of from five to ten minutes each time. Recognize it as both a food and an eliminator of poisons, as it is, and breathe, breathe, breathe, by Nature's method, and the lungs will distribute the oxygen to the blood, and the blood being the common carrier of the body will take it to all parts of the body and on its return will gather up all the waste and poisonous matters and will bring them to the lungs, where, meeting the fresh oxygen, they will be burned up and exhaled as carbonic acid gas, leaving the body pure and clean.

"The water you drink, in the proportion of three and one-half pints each day, is necessary in all adult bodies to insure perfect secretion and excretion. As the result of this required liquid being provided in normal quantity, the secreting glands will manufacture the proper amount of juices needed in digestion, absorption and assimilation of your food, and the excreting glands, those which bring about excretion or the removal of waste matters from the body—the liver giving you the bile, which produces a daily movement of the bowels—the kidneys and bladder removing the chemical deposits which come about through the processes of digestion, and the skin excreting a large amount of waste matter from its twelve square feet of surface, which you remove with a towel each morning after moistening it with cold water. By following these laws of Nature you will have a good appetite and digestion, a daily movement of the bowels, refreshing sleep, and, as your nutrition is restored from day to day, a feeling of satisfaction and happiness will be the result. Be earnest and persistent and do everything cheerfully, with a firm determination of doing your part to restore nutrition.

"When you breathe, give it the quality of your thought; it is for the purpose of getting food, life; feeding from the air and eliminating poisons from your body. (Repeat five and six times.) When you sip the water, think each time that it is to produce perfect secretion and excretion—to give you a good appetite, digestion, refreshing sleep and a free movement of the bowels each morning. (Repeat five or six times.) Each day look forward to the morrow for progress and advancement. Think health—talk it and nothing else. Do not talk with anyone about disease or allow any person to talk to you on such subjects. *Be cheerful, hopeful, confident* and fearless always, and you will be happy and healthy. Eat, drink, breathe and be merry."

It will be noticed that in the above described treatment, the suggestions are made along physiological and hygienic lines. That is, the suggestions indicate the physiological processes which are performed normally in the healthy person, the idea being to set up an ideal pattern for the Subconscious Mind to follow. In all scientific suggestive treatment the idea is always to paint a mental picture of the *desired conditions* rather than to dwell upon the existing undesirable conditions. The *ideal* is always held up to view, and the patient's mind is led to *realize* the ideal—to make the ideal real—to manifest the thought in action—to materialize the mental picture.

The general principles of Suggestive Therapeutics may be applied effectively by means of Auto-Suggestion. In fact, the "affirmations," "statements" and "assertions" used by many of the New Thought schools are but forms of Auto-Suggestion. There is no essential difference between the Suggestion given by others, and the Auto-Suggestion given by one's self to one's self. The healing power is in the mind of the patient, and whether it is called forth by his own Auto-Suggestion or the Suggestion of a healer matters not. The Auto-Suggestion is merely a case of self-healing by Suggestion, and is administered upon the principle of "every man his own suggestionist"—"sez I to meself, sez I." Auto-Suggestions are usually given to one's self in the form of "affirmations," as, "I am improving; my stomach is doing its work well, digesting what is given it, and the nourishment is assimilated, etc." In other works by the writer hereof, the method of addressing one's self as one would another is recommended as particularly efficacious. That is to say, instead of saying, "*I* am, etc.," in Auto-Suggestion, it is better to address one's self in the second person, as "*John Smith* (naming yourself), *you* are, etc." In short, the Auto-Suggestion seems to have additional force imparted to it by being directed as if it were being given to another person.

The following thought of Dr. Schofield is worthy of careful consideration in connection with the methods of applying Suggestion. He says, referring to the treatment of hysterical disorders and ailments: "We must, however, remember one great point with regard to suggestion—that it is like nitrogen. Nitrogen is the essential element in all animal life; it forms four-fifths of the air we breathe, and yet, curious to say, we have no power to use it in a pure state. We can only take it unconsciously, when combined with other substances in the form of proteid food. It is the same with suggestions. Not one hysterical sufferer in a hundred can receive and profit by them in a raw state—that is, consciously; they must generally be presented, as we have said, indirectly to the subconscious mind by the treatment and environment of the patient. An electric shock often cures slight hysterical diseases instantaneously, acting, as it often does, on the unconscious mind through the conscious. No doubt it would be easier if we could say to these sufferers, 'The disease is caused by suggestions from ideal centers, and to cure it, all you have to do is to believe you are well.' Still, it would be as impossible for us to take our nitrogen pure from the air, the mind cannot as a rule be thus acted on directly when the brain is unhealthy. Suggestion must be wrapped in objective treatment, directed ostensibly and vigorously to the simulated disease."

Not only is the above true regarding the treatment of hysterical disorders, but to *all* disorders as well. The methods which will bring about the best results must be carefully modeled upon the patient's particular temperament, education, prejudices for and against, and general belief. The skilled suggestionist adapts his treatment and methods to each individual case coming to him for treatment. Whatever method will best arouse the patient's belief, faith and expectant attention is the best method for administering the suggestions. The successful suggestionist must be "all things to all men," never, however, losing sight of the fundamental principle of Suggestion—the arousing of faith, belief, and expectant attention.

CHAPTER X

THE REACTION OF THE PHYSICAL

As we have stated in our Foreword, there is a constant action and reaction between the Mental States and the Physical Conditions. In this book, from the nature of our subject, we have started with the phase of the Mental State and worked from that point to the consideration of the Physical Condition. In the same way, many physiologists start from the phase of the Physical Condition, and work up to the Mental State. But, starting from either phase, the candid investigator must admit that there is an endless chain of action and reaction between Mind and Body—between Body and Mind.

This action and reaction works along the lines of building-up as well as tearing-down. For instance, if a person's Mental States are positive, optimistic, cheerful and uplifting, the body will respond and the Physical Conditions will improve. The Physical Conditions, thus improving, will react upon the Mental States giving them a clearness and strength greater than previously manifested. The improved Mental State again acts upon the Physical Conditions, improving the latter still further. And so on, an endless chain of cause and effect, each effect becoming a cause for a subsequent effect, and each cause arising from a preceding effect. Likewise, a depressed, harmful Mental State will act upon the Physical Conditions, which in turn will react upon the Mental States, and so on, in an endless chain of destructive cause and effect. It is a striking illustration of the old Biblical statement: "To him who hath shall be given; to him who hath not shall be taken away even that which he hath." In improving either the Mental State or the Physical Condition, one gives an uplift to the whole process of action and reaction; while, whatever adversely affects either Mental State or Physical Condition, starts into operation a depressing and destructive process of action and reaction. The ideal to be aimed at is, of course, "A healthy Mind in a healthy Body"—and the two are so closely related that what affects one, favorably or unfavorably, is sure to react upon the other.

Just as the influence of the Mental States over the Physical Conditions has been shown to operate by means of the Sympathetic Nervous System (controlled of course by the Subconscious Mind), so the influence of Physical Conditions over Mental States may be explained in physiological terms. In order to understand the reaction of the Body upon the Mind, we have but to recall the fact that the Subconscious Mind is the builder and preserver of the very brain-cells which are used by the Conscious Mind in manifesting thought. And also, that the entire Nervous System, both Cerebro-Spinal as well as Sympathetic, is really under the control of the Subconscious Mind so far as growth and nourishment is concerned. The very brain and nerve-centers in and through which is manifested thought, feeling, emotion, and will, are nourished by the Sympathetic System, and are hurt by anything affecting the latter. The Sympathetic System joins all parts of the organism so closely together that trouble in one part is reflected in other parts. Just as depressing thoughts will cause the organs to function improperly, so will the improper functioning of an organ tend to produce depressing thoughts.

Herbert A. Parkyn, M. D., well states the action and reaction of Mind and Body, as follows: "A tree is much like a human being. Give it plenty of fresh air, water and a rich soil, and it will flourish. In the same degree in which it is deprived of these does it wilt, and *the first part of the tree to wilt when the nutrition becomes imperfect is the top.* This is owing to the force of gravity; the blood of the tree, the sap, having to overcome this force of nature when nourishing the highest leaves. The blood of man is also affected by this same force, and the moment a man's circulation begins to run down, owing to stinted nutrition, we find that the first symptoms of trouble appear in the head.... The brain failing to receive its accustomed amount of blood, such troubles as impaired memory, inability to concentrate the attention, sleeplessness, nervousness, irritableness, the blues and slight headaches develop; and the impulses sent all over the body becoming feebler, the various organs do not perform their functions as satisfactorily as usual. The impulses to the stomach and bowels becoming weaker and weaker, dyspepsia, or constipation, or both, soon follow. As soon as these, the main organs of nutrition, are out of order, nutrition fails rapidly and more 'head symptoms' develop. Every impulse of the muscular system leaves the brain, and the strength of these impulses depends upon the nutrition to the brain centers controlling the various groups. As the nutrition to these centers declines, the whole muscular system, including the muscles of the bowels, becomes weaker and the patient complains that he exhausts easily. The impulses for elimination becoming weaker, waste products remain in the circulation, and any of the evils, which naturally follow this state of affairs, such as rheumatism, sick-headache, biliousness, etc., are likely to develop. The centers of the special senses feeling the lessening of the vital fluid, such troubles as impaired vision, impaired hearing, loss of appetite (sense of taste) and inability to detect odors quickly soon follow. The sense of touch becomes more acute, and it is for this reason that one in poor health becomes hypersensitive. Lowered circulation in the mucous membrane of the throat and nose is often the cause of nasal catarrh appearing on the scene as an early symptom."

It will thus be seen that the Physical Conditions, perhaps originally caused by depressing Mental States, have brought about a state of affairs in which the brain is imperfectly nourished and which consequently cannot think properly. The liver being out of order, the spirits are depressed; the brain being imperfectly nourished, the attention and will are weakened, and the patient finds it hard to use his mind to influence his bodily conditions. The bowels not moving properly, the waste-products poison the circulation, and the brain is unable to think clearly. In fact, the whole physical system is often so disturbed that a condition known as "nervous prostration" sets in, in which it is practically impossible for the patient to hold the Mental States which will improve the Physical Conditions. In these cases outside help is generally necessary, unless in cases where a sudden shock, or an urgent necessity arouses the latent mental forces of the individual, and he asserts the power that is in him, and begins to reverse the chain of cause and effect and to start on the upward climb.

The following additional quotation from Dr. Parkyn, gives us a vivid insight into the effect upon the Mental States of abnormal Physical Conditions: Dr. Parkyn says: "No organ of the body can perform its functions properly when the amount of blood supplied to it is insufficient, and we find, when the blood supply to the brain is not up to the normal standard, that brain functions are interfered with to a degree corresponding to the reduction in the circulation. Since the amount of blood normally supplied to the brain is lessened in nervous prostration, we find that the memory fails and the ability to concentrate the attention disappears. The reasoning power becomes weakened and the steadiest mind commences to vacillate. Fears and hallucinations of every description may fill the mind of a patient at this stage, and every impression he receives is likely to be greatly distorted or misconstrued. Melancholia with a constant fear of impending danger is often present. In fact, the brain seems to lose even the power to control its functions, and the mind becomes active day and night.... The reduction of the nutrition to the brain lessens the activity of all the cerebral centers also, and digestion becomes markedly impaired, thereby weakening the organ itself upon which the supply of vital force depends."

The physiologist is able to furnish a great variety of illustrations of the effect of Physical Conditions over Mental States. He shows that many cases of mental trouble are due to eye-strain, and other muscular disturbances, and that serious mental complaints sometimes arise by reason of physical lesions. The very terms used to designate certain abnormal mental states show the relation, as for instance, *melancholia* which is derived from the Greek words meaning "black bile"; and *hysteria*, which is derived from the Greek word meaning "the womb; or uterus." Every one knows the Mental States produced by a sluggish liver, or by dyspepsia, or from constipation. We all know the difference between our mental capacity for thinking when we are tired, as contrasted with that accompanying the refreshed physical condition. No man, whatever his philosophy, can truthfully claim to be able to maintain a placid, even disposition, and a perfectly controlled temper, when he is suffering from a boil on the back of his neck. And, all know that after indulging in the midnight "Welsh rarebit," one is apt to dream of his grandmother's ghost, or see dream elephants with wings. All know the delirium produced by overindulgence in liquor, and the hallucinations that accompany fever. The effect of drugs, tobacco, and alcohol upon the Mental States are well known. "Philip drunk" is a very different mentality from "Philip sober." The Mental States accompanying particular diseases are well known to physicians. One disease predisposes the sufferer to gloominess, while another will induce a state of feverish hilarity. Some leading authorities now hold that many cases of insanity are really due to abnormal conditions of the blood, rather than to any diseased condition of the brain.

One of the most marked instances of the action and reaction of Mental States and Physical Conditions is met with in the activities of the sexual organism. Psychologists very properly hold that sexual excesses and abnormalities are largely due to improper thinking, that is, by allowing the attention and interest to dwell too strongly and continuously upon subjects connected with the activities of that part of the physical system. Mental treatment along the lines of Suggestive Therapeutics has resulted in curing many persons of troubles of this sort. But, note the correlated fact—excess and abnormalities of the kind mentioned, almost invariably react upon the mentality of the person indulging in them, and softening of the brain, paralysis, or imbecility have often arisen directly from these physical abuses. It will be seen that any sane treatment of these troubles must take into consideration both Body and Mind. In the same way it is a fact that just as certain Mental States, notably those of fear, worry, grief, jealousy, etc., will injuriously affect the organs of digestion and assimilation, so will imperfect functioning of these organs tend to produce depressing mental states similar to those just mentioned. Many instances of the strange correspondences are met with in the study of physiological-psychology, or psychological-physiology.

In order to more fully appreciate the relation between the Body and the Mind, let us read the following lines from Prof. Halleck: "Marvelous as are the mind's achievements, we must note that it is as completely dependent upon the nervous system as is a plant upon sun, rain and air. Suppose a child of intelligent parents were ushered into the world without a nerve leading from his otherwise perfect brain to any portion of his body, with no optic nerve to transmit the glorious sensations from the eye, no auditory nerve to conduct the vibrations of the mother's voice, no tactile nerves to convey the touch of a hand, no olfactory nerve to rouse the brain with the delicate aroma from the orchards and the wild flowers in spring, no gustatory, thermal or muscular nerves. Could such a child live, as the years rolled on, the books of Shakespeare and of Milton would be opened in vain before the child's eyes. The wisest men might talk to him with utmost eloquence, all to no purpose. Nature could not whisper one of her inspiring truths into his deaf ear, could not light up that dark mind with a picture of the rainbow or of a human face. No matter how perfect might be the child's brain and his inherited capacity for mental activities, his faculties would remain for this life shrouded in Egyptian darkness. Perception could give memory nothing to retain, and thought could not weave her matchless fabrics without materials."

The very feelings or emotions themselves are so closely related to the accompanying physical expressions, that it is difficult to distinguish between cause and effect, or indeed to state positively which really is the cause of the other. Prof.

William James, in some of his works, strongly indicates this close relation, as for instance when he says: "The feeling, in the coarser emotions, result from the bodily expression.... My theory is that the bodily changes follow directly the perception of the exciting fact, and that our feeling of the same changes as they occur *is* the emotion.... Particular perceptions certainly do produce widespread bodily effects by a sort of immediate physical influence, antecedent to the arousal of an emotion or emotional idea.... Every one of the bodily changes, whatsoever it may be, is *felt*, acutely or obscurely, the moment it occurs.... If we fancy some strong emotion, and then try to abstract from our consciousness of it all the feelings of its bodily symptoms, we have nothing left behind.... A disembodied human emotion is a sheer nonentity. I do not say that it is a contradiction in the nature of things, or that pure spirits are necessarily condemned to cold intellectual lives; but I say that for *us* emotion disassociated from all bodily feelings is inconceivable. The more closely I scrutinize my states, the more persuaded I become that whatever 'coarse' affections and passions I have are in very truth constituted by, and made up of, those bodily changes which we ordinarily call their expression or consequence.... But our emotions must always be *inwardly* what they are, whatever may be the physiological ground of their apparition. If they are deep, pure, worthy, spiritual facts on any conceivable theory of their physiological source, they remain no less deep, more spiritual, and worthy of regard on this present sensational theory."

A deeper consideration of the relation between Mind and Body would necessitate our invading the field of metaphysical speculation, which we have expressed our intention to avoid doing. Enough for the purposes of our present consideration is: *the recognition that each individual is possessed of a mind and a material body; that these two phases or aspects of himself are closely related by an infinite variety of ties and filaments; that these two phases of his being act and react upon each other constantly and continuously; that in all considerations of the questiontion of either mental or physical well-being, or both, that both of these phases of being must be considered; that any system of therapeutics which ignores either of these phases, is necessarily "one-sided" and incomplete; and that, while, for convenience and clearness of specialized thinking, we may consider the Mind and the Body as separate and independent of each other, yet, we must, in the end, recognize their interdependence, mutual relation, action and reaction.*

Thus, the New Psychology recognizes the importance of the Body, while the New Physiology recognizes the importance of the Mind. And, in the end, we feel that both physiology and psychology must be recognized as being but two different phases of one great science—the Science of Life.